Under Her Wing

THE MENTORS WHO CHANGED OUR LIVES

BARBARA QUICK

New Harbinger Publications, Inc.

Author's Note

Some of the names and identifying circumstances of the interviewees have been changed to protect their privacy as well as that of their mentors.

Publisher's Note

This publication is designed to provide accurate and authoritative information in regard to the subject matter covered. It is sold with the understanding that the publisher is not engaged in rendering psychological, financial, legal, or other professional services. If expert assistance or counseling is needed, the services of a competent professional should be sought.

Distributed in the U.S.A. by Publishers Group West; in Canada by Raincoast Books; in Great Britain by Airlift Book Company, Ltd.; in South Africa by Real Books, Ltd.; in Australia by Boobook; and in New Zealand by Tandem Press.

Copyright © 2000 by Barbara Quick
New Harbinger Publications, Inc.
5674 Shattuck Avenue
Oakland, CA 94609

Cover design by Blue Design
Edited by Angela Watrous
Text design by Tracy Marie Powell

Library of Congress Catalog Card Number: 99-75292
ISBN 1-57224-197-7 Paperback

All Rights Reserved

Printed in Canada

New Harbinger Publications' Web site address: www.newharbinger.com

02   01   00

10   9   8   7   6   5   4   3   2   1

First printing

For my mother, Edie Tritel, who taught
me by her example that flowers can and do
bloom after forty

And to the memory of Jessica Mitford
(1917–1996), who so kindly and generously
took me under her wing

Also by Barbara Quick

Northern Edge: A Novel of Survival in Alaska's Arctic
Still Friends: Living Happily Ever After ... Even If Your
Marriage Falls Apart

Contents

Part I
Wanted: Fairy Godmother

Part II
Here's What You Get

Part III
Mentors, Fairy Godmothers, and Wicked Witches

Acknowledgements

I would like to thank Matthew McKay, Ph.D., who has been, at various times and over the course of many years, my employer, writing buddy, unpaid therapist, and now publisher. Without his encouragement, I don't think I would have taken the leap into nonfiction.

Angela Watrous, my editor at New Harbinger, was unrelenting in her demands and unwavering in her vision, causing me to produce a much better book than I would have if left to my own devices. She has both my respect and gratitude, as do Kristin Beck, Lauren Dockett, Gayle Zanca, and the rest of the staff at New Harbinger.

My metaphorical hat is off to Anita Goldstein and members of the Brain Exchange (www.thebrainexchange.com) for showing how women can and do help each other in a community context as well as one to one.

For her willingness to read whatever I'm writing, for her generosity in friendship and her enormous talent as a translator, Claudia Lenschen-Ramos has my warmest gratitude. I would also like to acknowledge the catalytic spark of enthusiasm expressed by Debbie Carton, reference librarian in the Berkeley Public Library system, when I queried her about the need for a book on this topic.

I am grateful to all the women who shared their insights and stories with me. *Under Her Wing* could never have been written without their contributions.

Both George and John have my unending thanks and love for their patience, understanding, encouragement, and readiness to be there for Julian when deadlines kept me at my computer.

And last but not least, Julian, my precious child, thank you for being exactly who you are.

Introduction

How It Started

The personal aspects of the mentor-protégée relationship hold a particular fascination for me. I've had two brilliant older women who took me under their wing in adulthood, and several other women who have served as role models to me and taken an interest in my work along the way. Most of these relationships have been quite wonderful; one of them went sour at the end. But each of them has represented an important link in my continuing evolution as a writer and a woman.

Although I had spent a lot of time thinking about these relationships in various contexts, I didn't truly understand them. What is it about one particular mentor-protégée dyad that makes it work beautifully, with mutual benefit to both parties, while another, equally promising relationship leaves both women feeling ill used? If we come to better understand the nature of these relationships, and enter into them with open eyes, can we ensure a greater frequency of happy endings? Why do some women hook up with a mentor, while others don't? Are there certain qualities or experiences that predispose a woman either to seek out a mentor or eventually become one; or is this a relationship that would be of great benefit to every woman?

Some time spent at the library proved that there is a gap in both the professional and trade literature on this topic. Very little has been written about the personal, psychological, and cultural content of the relationship between female mentors and their protégées. Paula J. Caplan provides an explanation for this in her book, *Don't Blame Mother:* "In fact, almost no systematic research has been conducted on woman-woman relationships of any kind; the funding for such research has simply not been available" (7).

When I set out to begin writing this book, I realized that I had no answers for my questions, and no sense about whether my own experiences would resonate at all for other women. I planned to interview women of diverse ages and from diverse backgrounds, but I had no idea whether any meaning or patterns would emerge when I had their stories all set down on paper.

With these uncertainties nagging at me, I set about trying to find at least thirty women to interview. My first surprise was that only about one in five of the women I queried said they'd had a female mentor (most said they would love to find one!). Every time I found another six or so people to interview, I set up a focus group at my house, promising tea-time snacks or supper, depending on the hour. I served cheese, crackers, and stuffed grape leaves, followed by pots of tea and chocolate chip cookies. I made giant pans of vegetarian lasagna, pots full of jambalaya, and enormous salads. Still wondering what in the world this book would be about, I ran the tape recorder, asked questions to keep the stories on track, kept the food and drinks flowing, and threw comments out to the group, hoping my interviewees would come up with answers to my larger questions and a framework for the book.

Many of the women said they'd never spoken to anyone else about their relationship with their mentor. Fortunately, I had lots of tissues on hand, as in each group, one or more of the women cried. After the second group poured their hearts out for two hours and said their goodbyes, I sat among the dirty dishes and half-filled glasses both emotionally exhausted and amazed.

There was a pattern, but it was not at all one I'd expected to find or had anticipated in any way, even in the long hours I'd given to thinking about my relationships with my own mentors.

In planning to write this book, I never expected to write about the mother-daughter relationship. And yet it seems that what women get from their female mentors is, in almost all cases, an idealized version of what girls are supposed to get from their mothers. A mentor gives us, in various combinations, acceptance and validation of our deepest sense of identity. She characteristically listens to us in a way we have never felt listened to before. And feeling witnessed by our mentors empowers us to be ourselves and pursue our dreams without fear.

What a mother gives that a mentor doesn't necessarily provide is—ideally—unconditional love. But in a certain way this seems to make the mentor's support and encouragement even more powerful. She is giving this to us because she sees our potential and believes in our ability—not because she is obligated to.

Some of the women I interviewed said explicitly that their mentors gave them what their mother failed to give them. For others, the mentor provided an alternative role model to that presented by their mother, empowering them to break family patterns and embark on a different path. For many, the mentor relationship afforded them the opportunity to complete developmental tasks they were unable to complete with their mother—although this was usually not explicitly stated as such, but either emerged in the interviews or was something that could be read later between the lines.

Another question I threw out to the groups—and which they grappled with and finally answered—had to do with defining the difference between someone you admire and someone who is your mentor. When is someone a role model, and when is she a mentor—and in what ways do these functions overlap?

One of the things I hoped to emerge with, when all was said and transcribed, was a set of guidelines for women who have not yet found a mentor, but long to form a relationship of this kind. Is this process something that can be deconstructed, so that any woman who wants a mentor can find one? Is there a cultural, biological, or even an evolutionary basis for a relationship of encouragement and support between an older and a younger woman, even those who are unrelated by blood? Or is the idea of female mentors simply an optimistic by-product of the women's movement?

In the course of interviewing some thirty women from widely divergent backgrounds and ranging in age from twenty-two to seventy-four, I stumbled upon answers to many of these questions. I also came to realize how interesting and important these questions are to our understanding of the ways in which human beings are sometimes able to work cooperatively and altruistically together. For it often seems that it is only cooperation and altruism that can possibly save us from destroying both our planet and ourselves.

There is nothing definitive about the conclusions drawn from these interviews. Perhaps, someday, better-trained observers with bigger budgets and a broader perspective will focus their attention on the whys and hows of the mentor-protégée relationship. This book was not generated from a scientific perspective. But even in the absence of broad survey research or theoretical principles, the words of the women who speak their hearts in these pages shine a great deal of light. There are common threads in these stories that tug at our heartstrings and jog our memories into recalling the mentors—perhaps long-forgotten—whose words and wisdom have helped us.

The Longing for a Mentor

No matter what culture we come from, in whatever place on earth, we grow up with certain pictures in our mind about what our lives may look like when we get older. These pictures are based both on things that are present and things that are absent in our lives.

I was one of those prissy girls who played with dolls a lot. I was good to my dolls. I combed their hair; I held tea parties for them on the carpeted floor of my grandmother's living room. And I think I was working out, through the orderly and nurturing world I created for my dolls and stuffed animals, an alternative reality to the sense of fear and instability that pervaded my childhood.

As I grew older, I was invariably drawn to older women—these were, at first, my friends' mothers—who were competent, nurturing, and powerful. Wendy's mother was a gourmet cook and a crack-shot conversationalist. In a rural paradise on the outskirts of Los Angeles, Megan's mother baked bread, kept goats, and was a published poet. Both these women were married to men who embodied for me everything that seemed kind, caring, and even noble in mankind—and I drank in the affectionate goodwill they showed me. Insinuating myself into my friends' homes, I felt comforted to know that there were alternatives to the unhappy life I saw my mother living. I was trying to figure out what the possibilities were for me when I grew up and became a woman.

Having these role models from outside my family—and also raiding the coffers of the novels I was constantly reading—I developed some pretty powerful pictures of what my future life might hold. I wanted to be beautiful or at least captivating, because I couldn't help but notice that, both in life and novels, it was the beautiful, captivating women who were always given the best prizes that life had to offer. I had no idea how I could ever transform myself from being the skinny, ugly child of the suburbs I saw myself as being to the sort of woman who is the toast of all Paris. But this type of glamorous attractiveness, I'm a little embarrassed to admit, was nonetheless high on my list of ambitions—I think mostly because of the power it seemed to confer.

I also felt that I had better manifest a tremendous talent, preferably in the arts. Throughout my girlhood, I dreamed of being an actress. I was good at a lot of things as a child (although not all that good at acting, despite years of training), and I had grown up believing myself only as good as my accomplishments. I had no inner, abiding sense that I was worthwhile, and that I deserved to be alive, simply on the basis of my existence in the world.

I left home at the age of seventeen to go to college with a good deal of emotional baggage and unfinished business. What I hadn't gotten as a girl I would have to find in my life as an adult. The most basic thing I lacked was the sense that who I was in the world was okay—and that I deserved to breathe the air I breathed and to take up the space I occupied on the planet.

I didn't look inside myself for the validation I needed, but to other people. For around twenty years, I tugged at the coattails of both men and women, wanting them to tell me that I was a good and lovable person. In this long, often tedious process, I was sometimes hurt terribly; and I also dealt out my own fair share of hurts, acting in a far less than lovable manner. I made enough errors in judgment for two or three different people.

Then, sometime after my fortieth birthday, everything changed for me. In my blind-sighted, stumbling way, leaving a trail of wrecked relationships in my wake, I'd managed to work through the unfinished developmental tasks that had traveled with me from childhood.

Ultimately, the knowledge that one is a worthy person has to take root on the inside. But my burgeoning self-esteem was given an infusion of water and light when Jessica Mitford, the famous muckraking journalist, agreed to read my first novel, *Northern Edge*.

I'd been commanded by my publisher to go out in search of jacket quotes from famous writers. When I first approached her, Jessica—who was known to all her friends and family as "Decca"—made a face and said no. She didn't "do" fiction, and she was terribly busy. She was sitting at a restaurant with her husband and some friends when I made my entreaty. I was noticeably pregnant. Wringing my hands, I said that it was a very short manuscript. Decca's friends elbowed her and said, "Come on, Decca, give her a break"—or something to this effect. Decca rolled her eyes and said in her basso profundo, "Oh, all right!"

A letter from Decca, containing the wonderfully flattering quote she provided for my book jacket, arrived just days after I'd had what was for both my husband and me a tragic fourth-month miscarriage. Decca not only loved the novel, but proposed that my husband and I come to a party at her house to be introduced to some of her friends.

From that time forward, until her death in 1996, Decca was my literary fairy godmother. She sent my book everywhere, including overseas to England to her sister, the Duchess of Devonshire. She called more than one book review editor, chivvying them into running a review of *Northern Edge*. I remember the flush of pleasure I experienced at one of her parties when someone introduced me to someone else as "Decca's protégée."

I was one of the people Decca called when she wanted a "date" for one of the literary or political outings her husband, Bob, couldn't attend. I became a back-up singer in a half-fictional, half-serious rock band Decca formed with the literary escort and producer Kathi Goldmark, called Decca and the Dectones. Along with Amy Tan and a host of other Bay Area writers with a sense of whimsy, we sang together on the rooftop of the Virgin Records Megastore in San Francisco. I took charge of Decca's cane while she gamely climbed the scaffolding leading onto the roof.

I have a photograph of Decca holding my son, Julian, in her arms a few weeks after he was born. I didn't notice it at the time, because I was caught up in nurturing both my child and a second novel, but there was a sore place inside me that began to heal under the influence of Decca's kindness to me. I don't want to suggest that we spent a good deal of time together or that I was in any way the only younger writer who benefited from her friendship. There was a whole flock of us. I saw Decca only once every couple of months or so. But our times together were precious to me. I would write about our meetings afterwards, recalling the stories she told me and always taking her advice, when she gave it, to heart.

What I'd been so fortunate to find was the unconditional goodwill of a mentor I both loved and admired. Decca was a brilliant *grande dame* of letters—a killingly funny writer who delighted in exposing the foibles of the pretentious and misinformed; a political activist who, unlike many others, was unwavering in her commitment to the causes she believed in even as she aged. She was the embodiment of the woman I'd dreamed of becoming when I was a young girl—brilliant, witty, beautiful in her time, and surrounded by a loyal following of family and friends.

In Decca's presence, under her wing and under her influence, I realized that I was both lovable, in my own way, and worthwhile. I will always delight in the validation other people are able to give me; but I no longer need that validation to know that the core of who I am inside is okay.

I tell my own story here simply to illustrate that a woman's longing for a mentor originates in childhood and can travel with her well into adulthood. In her essay "*Charlotte's Web*: Reading *Jane Eyre* Over Time," novelist Jane Lazarre writes of this yearning, "Especially if she has no woman to acknowledge her simple human virtue, her worth, she always carrie[s] around with her a secret that can sabotage her clarity, her energy, and her endurance" (235).

Iris, one of the women I interviewed, spoke about how a female mentor can provide women with a glimpse of a positive, hopeful future for themselves. Iris told me, "I've got enough negative models around my own age, but I want something positive to look forward to." If we don't see the future we want in the way our own mother is living her life, it is only natural for us to scan the horizon for an alternative model.

If we don't see such a model anywhere around us, we may move on to another, more promising territory. Page, a businesswoman in her forties, told me that she's been thinking a great deal about whether she should move back to the east coast, where she grew up:

> *It breaks my heart to think about leaving, because I have a wonderful community of friends here. But all of them are around my own age. What I'm really missing here is older women in my life to offer me guidance. Part of the pull to go back east is that I have relatives and family there, and older women from my hometown who I know would be in my life there. I'd be able to form some sort of picture of how to live my future.*

Maria is a physician in her late thirties who grew up feeling like there was something wrong with her, because everything she wanted was so different from what others said she was supposed to want:

> *Sometimes I would just pray that whatever aliens had left me here would just come back and take me away with them. I liked girls—not boys. I wanted to be a doctor—not a nurse or a teacher or a mommy. All my cousins and both my sisters dropped out of school to start families. I knew my mother loved me, but I never felt that she could in any way understand who I was*

inside— because what I am is so completely different from what she is and what she's always known. When I tried to imagine my future, there were just no models to put into the picture. Now I can see what it looks like, but only because I've had to paint this picture from scratch. There were no numbers to follow, no outlines to fill in.

Paula, a therapist, believes that the longing for a mentor is connected not only to our need for validation, but also to the need that girls often feel to justify their own sense of power and ambition:

Boys grow up knowing that they're supposed to "go for it" in terms of whatever they want physically or professionally. Ambition and drive—pulling themselves up by their bootstraps, being a self-made man, eviscerating the competition—all of these qualities are applauded by society when they're exhibited by a boy.

I'll never forget telling my grandfather, who I adored, that I'd made plans to deliver a car cross-country, then take a Russian steamer to Ireland, where I hoped to live for a year or two. "Isn't that wonderful?" I asked him. "Isn't it exciting?" I could see the conflicting emotions in his face when he answered me—part of him was simply thrilled for me, but another part was terribly frightened, because he loved me so much and wanted to protect me. He had tears in his eyes when he finally said, "It would be, for a boy."

Things have changed somewhat since then, I hope. But I know that I was constantly on the lookout for powerful women who in effect would give me permission

to feel as powerful and strong and ambitious as I felt
myself to be—and to still feel like a woman in every
way.

Why Women Need Female Mentors

Paula's insights are borne out by the latest scientific research. In his essay "Sex Stereotypes: An Underlying Dimension," sociologist Lloyd P. Lueptow surveys research on sex stereotypes and discusses how our notions about masculine and feminine traits and behavior have remained unchanged from the 1950s in the United States and across cultures. Lueptow comments on how remarkable this is, especially when considered in the light of changes in sex roles and sex-role orientations that occurred during the latter half of the twentieth century.

On the one hand, we grow up believing that we should accomplish great things in the outside world. On the other hand, we're weighed down by gender stereotypes in the personal realm that haven't kept pace with changes in the worlds of work and career. Sarabeth, a research chemist, commented, "Somehow, we're supposed to do it all: to be at the forefront of cutting edge research and also to be able to drop everything at a moment's notice and give a dinner party that would do Martha Stewart proud!"

Research cited in Lueptow's essay found that people who have what are traditionally considered to be masculine traits—assertiveness, strength, independence, and objectivity—tend to have the best psychological adjustment, whether they're male or female.

Boys can look all around them and find role models who are in full possession of their masculinity. It's the very characteristics of maleness that lead, in our society, to success. Girls, on the other hand, have a much smaller pool of potential mentors. We look at the majority of women around us and see expressiveness, support, and emotionality—none of which are associated with the traditional route to the achievement of goals or the promotion of ambitions. Although these more stereotypical feminine traits actually do have great value, their effects are less easily translated into the many situations still largely governed by masculine ideals.

This is why women need female mentors. Whether based on culture, biology, or a combination of both, our notions of what it means to be female have not caught up with the sense of power, and the expansiveness of the ambition, that women of all ages can sometimes feel. Society does not give us permission to feel this way and still feel "feminine." Lueptow points out that these stereotypes have prevailed despite the fact that parents have dramatically changed their attitudes about what is appropriate for little boys and girls. Even though today most little boys are given dolls to play with in addition to their toy trucks, and most little girls are encouraged to join a sports team and play games other than "house," gender stereotypes continue to be played out in real life.

If a boy's father comes up short, there are many other places he can look in society for a role model. But because what it means to be a successful woman has grown so complex, a girl may have to search far and wide before she finds a role model who balances all these traits—both the traditionally masculine and feminine—successfully. For many of us, the challenge is finding a way to embrace our ambitions without compromising our more feminine qualities.

Kirin, a corporate vice president, talked about how she has tried to avoid going overboard in adapting the traits that are considered masculine:

> *A lot of the women who rise to the upper reaches of the corporate world do so by being even meaner and more cutthroat than the men. That's not what I wanted for myself. I'm unwilling to sacrifice who I am at heart on the altar of success. But I do want success—that's also very much a part of who I am. I realize how lucky I was to be taken under the wing of someone who is able to be incredibly tough and incredibly nurturing at the same time.*

Claiming Your Wings

I found, in writing this book, that the voices of the various mentors discussed here echoed in my head at odd hours of the day or night whenever I felt worried or discouraged. When my worry was at its height, I heard Sarabeth's mentor, Ruth, saying, "Stay focused on what you are doing. Don't try to sew up your entire future now." There was an echo of Kirin's mentor, who said to her, "You might feel like giving up. But if you stay with it, you'll be amazed at what you're capable of doing." Kate's mentor whispered, as if over a distant telephone line, "You're my precious girl."

Working to the accompaniment of this chorus of encouraging voices, I realized that we all have inside of us an inner mentor. Some of us are fortunate enough in our lives to be brought up by or, later, nurtured by a kind, wise, and loving woman who gives us tools that will help guide and hearten us during our entire walk on this planet.

The novelist Diane Leslie wrote to me, "I guess I got my mentoring from books. If I had a guide through hard times, I'm almost embarrassed to say, it was an imaginary mentor—someone I made up during my youth." In her 1999 novel, *Fleur de Leigh's Life of Crime,* Diane creates a wondrous mentor for her lonely young protagonist. Thea Roy, an aged star from the days of silent films, advises the much-neglected Fleur, "Make use of your misery, that's my motto." Later in the story, she tells Fleur, "If you want the best, you must give it." When the young Fleur asks the aged Thea why she's never had a face-lift, Thea responds, "Me? I'm proud of the lines on my face. Every one of them tells a story, and together they prove I've *lived.*"

It's the special privilege of fiction writers to create such delightful role models out of the longings of their imaginations. But it's the sad truth that most women, at least at this time in our history and in our culture, do not have a female mentor, not even an imaginary one.

In making my initial queries, I noticed that the absence of a mentor is a source of sorrow for many women. To all those who have not yet found the fairy god-mother of their dreams, know that it's never too late for this to happen. Our mentor's face may, if we're very lucky, be the first face we see when we enter the world; but there is just as great a chance that it will be a face we'll encounter much later in our lives. Kate, one of the women interviewed for this book, was in her sixties when her mentor appeared to help and heal her.

In the meantime, though, all of us can benefit by tapping in to the wisdom, kindness, and generosity of the mentors recalled here. If we listen closely enough, we can hear an echo of their voices inside us.

We are certainly more than our own individual selves. There is a collective consciousness that sings through our cells as human beings; and there is a collective wisdom that sings through our cells as women. We have a history of helping each other, from the time when the first woman helped another as she gave birth, or shared her stash of nuts and berries while another nursed her child.

By tapping into this legacy, we are empowered—as all the women in this book have been in their lives—to fulfill our potential and inhabit our true identities. You don't have to have a mentor outside your own mind to reap the enormous benefits of being taken under her wing. They're your wings as well. All you have to do is claim them.

Part I

Wanted:
Fairy Godmother

1

*Do You Carry
Mentors Here?*

The mentor nurtures your spirit, or your capacity as a person. There are elements of that that may have to do with who you are, or who you truly could be, or how you want to be in the world, or what you want to do. And there are all different kinds of ways in which those qualities or possibilities can be nurtured.

—*Violetta*

I guess going up to someone, as an adult, and saying, "Will you be my mentor?" is sort of like going up to a guy and saying, "Will you be my boyfriend?" There's an outside chance that you'll just fall into each other's arms and live happily ever after; but it's far more likely that you'll get looked at like you're some kind of weirdo.

—*Cathy*

I think you have the kind of mentor who is the rainmaker, who makes the opportunities for you, and you have the kind of mentor like my grandmother, who opens doors inside you.

—*Dorothy*

What girl has heard the story of Cinderella without wishing that *she* had a fairy godmother who would magically appear in times of need? You don't have to be as miserable or exploited as Cinderella to need a fairy godmother—every girl needs one. It's a well-kept secret, but every woman needs one, too.

We tend, as women, to focus on our need for the love of our life to come along and ensure that we live happily ever after. But, in truth, the succor provided by the prince at the end of *Cinderella* is no more than a presumption. We're told that the newly married couple lived happily ever after. But we're given absolutely no indication about the content of that happiness—apart from the inference that Cinderella will no longer have to do a lot of housework.

Does the fairy godmother, like a family doctor, remain on call after the fairy tale ends? She's the one, after all, who gave Cinderella the self-confidence and moxie—to say nothing of the wardrobe and the transportation—that allowed her to make her conquest at the ball.

Although *Cinderella* is usually seen as a love story, it is also the story of a young woman and her mentor. Cinderella, who has been coping fairly well up to this time (considering the circumstances!), is faced with a crisis. In order to move on to the next stage in her career (i.e., to go to the ball), she has to, in effect, become a version of herself that has only existed heretofore in her imagination. Cinderella knows what she needs—and a modern-day woman might read this as more education, a kick in the butt, and a new image. But she needs help if these changes are going to come about in time for her to get to the ball properly decked out.

Enter the fairy godmother, who sizes up the situation, waves her magic wand, and says some empowering words. "Of course you can get your Ph.D.," she tells Cinderella, "and at one of the better schools, too!" In a shower of fairy dust, Cinderella's true self becomes visible for the first time since her wicked stepmother assumed control of the household. The beautiful and powerful personage Cinderella always knew herself to be, despite her rags and the dirt under her fingernails, suddenly becomes manifest.

The main reason this happens is because her fairy godmother saw through the rags and the dirt to Cinderella's innermost identity: she witnessed Cinderella, and in so witnessing her, she made it possible for Cinderella to fully become herself.

In the story, it's Cinderella's need that brings her mentor to her. But how do women and girls outside the realm of fairy tales find a fairy godmother of their own? There isn't a mentor store you can go to. There is a web site—www.mentoring.org—which can give you tips for either finding or becoming a mentor. But the site, sponsored by the National Mentoring Partnership, is exclusively designed to serve the mentoring needs of people under eighteen years of age. There's useful information here, including a bulletin board; but chances are that if you're older than Cinderella was, you won't find a mentor there.

An increasing number of corporations support mentorships among their employees, and even the State of California funds a mentoring program. Such programs are designed to match junior workers to more experienced people in their field who can foster their career success. But institutional or corporate mentoring is usually something quite distinct from the phenomenon described in Cinderella and in the stories throughout this book. What causes the magical transformations that result from the relationship between a mentor and her protégée? And how do we go about finding that woman with a magic wand?

Far more women want a mentor than have one. Terry, a thirty-something management consultant, says that she just hasn't found, or been found by, that sparkling, wonderful older woman who could lend her help in facing her problems or making better decisions at life's crossroads. Terry told me:

> *Throughout my life—high school, college, career, and life in general—I've had various people who have been in mentor roles for brief periods of time. But there's been no one person who's really turned me on a different path or was there to validate the decisions I've made—no one I could, say, call on the phone now and thank for all she's done. I have a certain sadness about that, and a certain sense that, gosh, maybe it's something I should have done or looked for.*

Matchmaking services sometimes do the trick when it comes to a person's search for a romantic partner. But most happy couples, when queried, have a story to tell about the strange and wonderful way in which they met. It was kismet, it was chance, it was plain, dumb luck. As you'll read in the stories here, finding the mentor of your dreams bears a striking similarity to the search for love.

The shortest route, of course, is through your family. If your mother or another relative happens to be the right match to serve as a mentor for you, you don't have to look further than your own front door.

Outside your circle of family and friends, mentors tend to be found in exactly the same places as potential romantic partners—at work, at school, at church, or in any social groups you belong to. You can never really tell where you'll find a mentor, just as you can never accurately predict where and when you'll fall in love. The key, in both cases, seems to be your readiness for the experience, which sends out a sort of radar to the world.

Nonetheless, lots of people who say they would love to be in a relationship project something that tells potential partners to keep their distance. If this were not true, there wouldn't be so many lonely people around! By the same token, women who are ready to receive the guidance, help, and nurturing of a mentor are more likely to find one.

Paula, a therapist, told me:

> *I really do believe that we get what we want in life. Our main problem is in understanding what we want, and in being able to actualize it by forming clear pictures in our minds. I'm not saying that we can have anything we want just by imagining it—but I do think that daydreaming is a very important aspect of understanding our needs and the ways in which we might fulfill them. Recognizing a sore or empty place in your life that could be healed by a mentor is the first step toward finding one. You'll be more attuned to all the potential helpers around you.*

There is, alas, no one way to find a mentor of the fairy godmother variety, no formula or book of rules you can follow. But in reading the stories here, you'll probably find some clues that will help you along your way if you're looking for a mentor. If you have a mentor already or if you *are* a mentor, you'll learn more about how this magical process works.

What Is a Mentor, Anyway?

A female mentor is defined more by what she gives us than by who she is. Mothers can be mentors to their daughters. Grandmothers, aunts, and sisters can also be mentors. Teachers are, very definitely, an active part of the mentor pool. A mentor doesn't even need to be older than you are; she may simply have some knowledge or wisdom, along with the will to help you.

Our mentors use magic wands—their influence or their wisdom—to gain us entry to the ball, the graduate program, the career, or the life path of our dreams. But besides working their magic, they also enhance our lives with their love.

Rita, a primary schoolteacher and teacher trainer, expressed her belief that love is at the heart of the mentor-protégée relationship. Speaking of a mentor who runs a Buddhist discussion group she belongs to, Rita told me, "I really love her, and it's that love connection that allows me to admire her and want to please her and want to know that she understands where I'm coming from—all the while letting her know that I appreciate what she offers."

Our mentors also give us hope. Iris, a pattern-maker for a high-fashion designer, has just reached the age of thirty. Iris has grappled with the definition of a female mentor:

I think, for me, I would want a mentor who'd be able to give me some direction, be it spiritual or professional. But I think also I want somebody to give me hope that my future is going to be fulfilling. When I see women who are older than I am, who are finding fulfillment still, that's when I have hope that life is not so hard on women that it's crushing, you know? That's when I feel that I'll still be able to keep going, even during those times when life can seem really hard.

How we define a mentor seems to depend, to a large extent, on our own experiences. Kirin, who is now a corporate vice president, was taken under the wing of an older woman at the first corporation she worked for, where she had an entry-level management position. Kirin told me, "There is by definition a power differential between a mentor and her protégée. A mentor necessarily has to be someone who is elevated above you in terms of her hierarchical power."

Simone, a graduate student in French literature, thinks of a mentor as someone who is tough with you while keeping your best interests at heart. Simone explained:

She's somebody who says, "You can do this! I don't want to hear any arguments about it." In my case, both of my mentors pushed me to do what I was afraid of doing, but wanted to do. They helped me claim my ambition, my belief in myself. I'm not at all sure how that process happens.

Page has been looking for a mentor. She found one briefly in the business realm, when she was starting her own business. But now she wants to connect with a woman who can give her some spiritual guidance as well. Her definition of a mentor expresses what she'd like to find in one: "I think what a woman looks for in a mentor is someone who can witness her and see her for who she is, and then guide her only insofar as she is validating her strengths."

Dorothy is a retired benefits manager who is working on her first novel. When she was three years old, Dorothy was taken under the wing of her paternal grandmother, who stepped in to take care of her when Dorothy's parents were declared unfit by the courts. Dorothy offered a definition of the difference between an organizational mentor and a mentor of the heart:

> *A mentor is someone who takes an active interest in you as a person, recognizes some germ of potential there, and nurtures it. What I think of as a formal mentor can help you find your way along and very definitely open doors for you, or have something to do with pulling strings to help you get where you need to go. They recognize, once the door is open for you, that you have the potential and the qualifications to take advantage of that opportunity. I think you have the kind of mentor who is the rainmaker, who makes the opportunities for you, and you have the kind of mentor like my grandmother, who opens doors inside you.*

Ursula, an artist and graphic designer, found her first mentor in her mother. She says that she saw her mother, who is also an artist, as her mentor from the very beginning:

> *I was sort of in love with my mother. I mean, I thought my mother was great, and my mother was*

*young—and tough. She ran around barefoot once we got
up to the farm, and the bottoms of her feet were so tough
that she could put a cigarette out with her heel. She
went to square dances. She took me and my sisters everywhere. We had a great library, and I read all the time.
I was encouraged to read. I was encouraged to make
things. I was given sketchpads. We had a garden, and
we worked in it together. It was a very positive lifestyle
in many ways, and it gave me a lot to build on in my
life, later on. I had this model of a tough, strong, talented
woman who also really cared about me in every way.*

Weighing in with yet another opinion, Violetta, who's
getting a Ph.D. in math education, feels that formal or institutional mentorships can also partake of that strong heart
connection. Violetta drew on her own very positive and
meaningful relationship with a female academic mentor
who has known Violetta since she was eighteen:

*There's a certain personal-professional mix that I think
can only really develop over time. It takes a certain
amount of trust on the part of both people when you're
both willing to be seen as whole human beings. A
mentor can help you see and accept yourself, but it's also
reciprocal. Over time, she'll reveal her own strengths and
weaknesses. In terms of the mentors I've worked with,
there's been a bi-directional learning, as far as the
personal interaction that was going on. I was never just
a student, and they weren't just a professor or an
advisor.*

*I think the common thread in any kind of
meaningful mentor relationship has to do with a kind of*

nurturing. The mentor nurtures your spirit, or your capacity as a person. There are elements of that that may have to do with who you are, or who you truly could be, or how you want to be in the world, or what you want to do. And there are all different kinds of ways in which those qualities or possibilities can be nurtured. I don't think you can carve it off into two separate things. That makes it seem somehow that my work is just a job, that it can stand separate from who I am as a person. But I don't actually feel that way, because what I do is very much related to who I am.

Cathy, a paralegal, expressed the belief that it is circumstances, more than anything else, that create mentors:

I really think there's some kind of projection going on, because we find in our mentors what we'd really like to see in ourselves. Only maybe it's really hard, for whatever reason at that moment or in those circumstances, to see it in yourself. So you find this strength or encouragement or nurturing—or whatever it is that you need at that moment—in this other woman, in this person outside yourself who's also a little bit like you, only older maybe, and more successful or established or whatever.

I think we sometimes only recognize our mentors in retrospect, because you can see what they've given you after the fact, and you can look back and see the influence they've had on your life.

A mentor is like cable to the TV sets of our interior landscapes—an outside connection providing sudden and miraculous clarity. Caryn, a high school biology teacher, told me:

> *In my own relationship with the mentor I had when*
> *I was getting my master's degree, it was sort of a*
> *sensitive period for me. It was a critical point in*
> *time when I was dealing with a lot of different and*
> *sometimes conflicting issues—finishing my degree and*
> *whether I should put off having children, and then*
> *some sort of painful stuff about whether I had made*
> *the right choices about what to do with my life. The*
> *relationship I had with my mentor allowed a lot of*
> *these things to gel for me, and to become much clearer.*

Pardon Me, But Are You a Role Model or a Mentor?

What is the difference between someone you admire very much and someone who is a mentor? Rita told me:

> *I guess you can admire somebody that doesn't even*
> *know you exist. Or you can admire somebody that*
> *you've worked with, but there isn't any—I'm not sure*
> *how to say it—heart touch between you. I don't know*
> *that you both need to know what the relationship*
> *means to you. I don't think my auntie would have*
> *ever thought of herself as a mentor. But she certainly*
> *was a mentor for me, even though I wasn't able to*
> *think of the relationship in that way until many,*
> *many years later. She was simply my auntie, and*
> *someone I very much admired.*

Caryn feels that admiration isn't the key to defining this relationship:

You can admire a character in literature or a character in a movie, or all sorts of things—a historical character. And maybe if you don't have a mentor in real life, this kind of imaginary mentor may be the next best thing. I mean, that's why we read history, or one of the reasons, isn't it? It can be a way of creating in advance, in a way, the qualities of the mentor you'd like to find. But it's a different kind of relationship altogether, because it's one-way. There's no reciprocity.

Rita adds, "Your mentor has to have some impact or something that would allow some kind of change to happen in you."

In Carol's experience, a mentorship involves education of some kind: "I don't mean education in a formal way, but in the sense that your mentor is teaching you something, even if what she's teaching you is entirely about yourself. But it's an active relationship. Your mentor takes an active part in helping you become who you're going to be."

Dorothy speculated about the distinctions between a role model and a mentor:

In trying to think about who my mentors have been and what I was going to say, I wasn't sure that my story would have anything to do with the subject of this book, because my grandmother had no education. She picked cotton for a living. With a role model you can say, "Oh, she's a television broadcaster, and so I want to be a television broadcaster like her." You've seen somebody who has made this thing happen in her life, and so you figure you can follow in those footsteps. That would be the role model. And that would be somebody that you just see on TV. You don't know them; they don't know you.

But the mentor, I think, is someone who takes an active interest in you as a person, recognizes some germ of potential there, and nurtures it. So I thought about my grandmother, who was this barely literate person, but she taught me. She was able to take me by the hand and teach me her values, and just kind of inculcate me with the idea that you need an education, you need to be independent, those sorts of things—and you can definitely do it, and I'll be with you every step of the way.

She had no idea what any of this meant in the way that a formal mentor would. A formal mentor knows the actual steps that you have to take, and they can help you find your way along and very definitely open doors for you or pull strings to help you get where you need to go. So I think that you have the kind of mentor who makes the opportunities for you, and you have the kind of mentor like my grandmother, who didn't have a clue. She was most definitely a mentor to me, but in terms of what she actually did in her life, and what I wound up doing, she wasn't by any stretch of the imagination what you could call a role model.

Marcella offered a short definition of the differences between a mentor and a role model: "One relationship is reciprocal, and the other one is not. The mentor-protégée relationship is reciprocal. A role model doesn't even have to know you exist."

But a mentor can also be a role model. Simone told me:

I became very close to this professor who had been my mentor. I have to admit that I admire her totally. Basically, I want to be her, you know? I want to be as bright as she is. I hope to be as bright as she is. She's very accomplished. She writes articles and goes to all these conferences, and is invited everywhere. The way she is, it's exactly what I would like to be.

Charlotte's mentor also served as a role model for her, demonstrating a way of life that was quite different from the lifestyle Charlotte had seen growing up in the Midwest. Charlotte was in her early twenties, in her first job, when she and her mentor crossed paths:

I would come over, and Jackie's partner, Tom, would be there. She was kind of a model for me of alternative lifestyles, so her influence went beyond just my career.

I come from Indiana, and people are very conventional there. I've never been that way, but I never had any alternative models like that. Jackie embodied the possibilities for living a way of life that was the way I wanted to live. She and Tom weren't married. They didn't see any need to get married, and I always had that kind of feeling about marriage, too. Here I finally had this real-life example of an alternate lifestyle to getting married, having babies, you know, the whole bit.

For Ursula, the functions of mentors and role models have always overlapped. "All the women that I think of as mentors are older than I am, so there's a wisdom that they have that I don't have yet, and I recognize that. Their wisdom draws me to them, as well as their identity—who they are as people."

Elizabeth Kamarck Minnich found a powerful role model, as well as a mentor, in Hannah Arendt. In her essay, *"Hannah Arendt: Thinking as We Are,"* Minnich wrote, "The courage she showed in speaking and in withstanding the sometimes intense reaction to her thought gave me a picture of courage to hang on to; she was living proof that genuine thinkers cannot retreat from the real work, the real action of politics" (173).

Violetta disliked the idea of her story being placed exclusively in the context of a professional category of mentorship. Speaking of her mentor, she said, "I happened to have met her in that capacity, but the impact our relationship has had on my life is way bigger than my profession."

Dorothy observed:

> *Within the category of personal mentors, there do seem to be the type who are in your field, and then there's somebody, you know, who's more connected to your heart exclusively—someone who's not in your field, and maybe instead of opening doors in the outside world for you, she's helping you open inner doors. Maybe that's one way to distinguish it, although it sounds like there are those mentors who are able to open both kinds of doors, both on the inside and on the outside, too. So a role model is not necessarily a mentor, but a mentor can certainly be a role model.*

Paula also had some thoughts on this distinction:

> *In defining a role model, I think the focus is on that other person's identity, not on yours. You might want to*

be just like that person with all your heart, but there's no mapping out of the way to get there—and there may be thousands of metaphorical miles and all sorts of obstacles between where you are now and where she is. I might want to be, oh, I don't know, Audrey Hepburn, or Eleanor Roosevelt, or even Mother Teresa. But there's just no way I can be any of those women, because I'm myself, not them.

In defining a mentor, I think the focus is more on you and your aspirations, on your strengths and your goals. The mentor's focus is on you and how you can reach your goals. Now if your mentor happens to be Audrey Hepburn or Eleanor Roosevelt or Mother Teresa—well, then the two functions just perfectly coincide.

How Do You Find a Mentor?

The guidelines given by the National Mentoring Partnership for finding a mentor can certainly be extrapolated for adults. On their web site (www.mentoring.org) they tell young people what to look for with any mentor:

Someone who believes in you and will go to bat for you. Someone who will tell you the truth. Someone who's not afraid of hard work. Someone who cares about doing the right thing. Someone you can trust . . .

Make some notes about what you'd like to get out of a mentoring relationship. It is easier to ask someone for help if you yourself know what you are asking for.

> *Make a list of all the people you know who might be able to be your mentor or to help you find a mentor. Be sure to consider the full range of possibilities, including family, friends, neighbors, teachers, coaches, club leaders, ministers, and others. Think about what things different people can help you with.*
>
> *Think about how you might approach them. You may want to call on the telephone and arrange a time to meet and talk in person. Or, you may want to stop by in an informal way. Ask if this is a convenient time to talk to them for a few minutes and ask for their help.*
>
> *Ask them to be your mentor or to help you find a mentor.*

Setting out to find a mentor can be just as frightening for an adult as it is for a teenager—maybe more so. As anyone in sales knows, you have to have a pretty tough skin if your work involves making "cold calls." Actively seeking a mentor may increase your chances of finding one. But you'll have to steel yourself to the possibility of rejection, bearing in mind that your quest may take a long time and many tries.

Page called her minister on the phone, asking if she would be her mentor, and was answered with a curt "I can meet with you, but only for fifteen minutes."

In some ways, it can feel unnatural to ask someone to be your mentor. Cathy says:

> *I guess going up to someone, as an adult, and saying, "Will you be my mentor?" is sort of like going up to a guy and saying, "Will you be my boyfriend?"*

There's an outside chance that you'll just fall into each other's arms and live happily ever after; but it's far more likely that you'll get looked at like you're some kind of weirdo.

Just asking a question like that makes you very vulnerable, because most people are just unwilling to have their personal space encroached upon in that way. I think it's sort of like the boyfriend thing. The mentor likes it better when they get to make the first move— you know, scope you out first and identify you as someone they're interested in. I think a lot of mentoring relationships start that way, at least for adults—I know mine did, with Sam. She definitely thought of the idea of coaching me and helping me at a time when it wouldn't have even entered my consciousness that she might have taken the slightest interest in me at all.

Although Penny was in junior high school when she met her first mentor, the pattern of the relationship followed the model that Cathy described. Penny said:

I had this English teacher, Mrs. Wood, and she was great. She was very butch, and she wore polyester pantsuits, and she had a real sort of severity. I remember walking into her class the first time and just being scared to death of her. But she was very warm to her students and very supportive of them.

We began to have sort of a relationship because she liked the things that I wrote. She would give me special assignments and told me about Hemingway, and we started reading some of the Victorian literature at an earlier age than some of my contemporaries were.

She really made me feel very special about my ability as a writer. And she also just had that sort of older woman, strong, unaffected-by-the-culture essence about her, do you know what I mean? I remember taking note of that at a really early age. I don't know that I still wasn't affected by the pressures of being a young girl. But she at least was able to help me see that I had these talents as well—to remember those.

Like Penny, Terry also found a mentor at school:

I don't advocate gymnastics for young women these days; I wouldn't want my own daughters to go into it in any serious way, because the sport has really changed. But back then it was really lovely. Junior high had been a painful period for me. Not socially, just, you know, the usual things— pimples, braces. Coming out of that and finding gymnastics in high school was really wonderful.

Mrs. Watkins, the coach, had gone to Penn State, and she was a phys ed major. She was really attractive. She was the swimming coach and the gymnastics coach and the something else coach. She was a role model for a lot of girls at the high school, and she took a special interest in me when I was in the eleventh grade. She actually helped me get a gymnastics scholarship at a small liberal arts college, which I was very excited about.

The team was a nice group, and Mrs. Watkins really kind of embodied that philosophy that it's not if you win or lose, it's how you play the game. Of course, she wanted us to win; but she was really lovely about it. We weren't as cutthroat or nasty as the other gymnastics

*clubs. So she really provided a great role model for us,
and she was a powerful mentor for me for a while.*

Betsy made a direct approach in contacting her mentor, although she had no idea that the famous painter—whom Betsy had chosen as the subject for her Master's thesis—would become a mentor to her:

*I think I saw something that I admired and wanted
to emulate in some of her work. And I approached
her simply by writing her a letter. She was very
approachable, I now know, but I had no idea at the
time whether or how I would be received. I just wrote
her a letter and asked if I could go over and interview
her. And she just said, "Oh, fine." Anyway, I made
an appointment to go over and see her at her home,
and we did a series of interviews, which I tape recorded
and used as a basis for my thesis.*

Thirty-three-year-old Simone has had two powerful mentors, both of whom eased her way into the academic world:

*When I moved here from France, I wasn't very
interested in being in connection with anybody from my
country. But after I had a little girl, I started to think
that I should probably get more in touch with people
who spoke French, because I wanted her to speak
French. All my family is back in France, and none of
them speak English. So I responded to a little ad I saw
in a newsletter from the French Consul or something—
I really don't remember the details. There was someone
who was looking for a person to join a little French*

theater, a cabaret troupe. So I went to this woman's house; she was a retired law professor, and the complete opposite of what I was in terms of class

There's a lot of social consciousness among French people. I come from a blue-collar background. Both my parents had quit school when they were thirteen. My mother was a stay-home mom, caring for seven children when I was growing up. And my father was a mechanic with no formal education. I did go to and graduate from high school. I went on to a public university in France for about two years. I was very upset about not being able to finish school.

After having joined the workforce in France, Simone got the idea of moving to California to finish her education and escape what she saw as her blue-collar destiny. But soon after her arrival in the States, she married and had a child. She was twenty-three at the time:

I was really not happy with what was happening to me, because I just felt I was following a script that had been written for me before I was born. Nobody expected me to even go to school or finish college. I was just the textbook example that you read about in studies of what happens to kids from blue-collar families. They will be blue collar, and they will repeat the same thing over and over.

The woman who eventually became my first mentor was from a very aristocratic family that had a lot of money. I remember her telling me that she had gotten her Ph.D. when she had five kids, and that I had no excuse. At that point, I thought, well, you

*know, it's easy for you, even with five children. You had
money. I just couldn't relate to her socially.*

Simone was eventually brought around to seeing her
own social prejudices, and the ways in which these were
causing her to sabotage her academic ambitions: "My mentor changed a lot of my opinions and opened up my eyes to
what I should be doing. She just talked to me, didn't force
me into anything; but eventually the fact that I had responded
to that little ad completely turned my life around."

Charlotte was in her early twenties when she met her
mentor:

*I had a job at this Washington, D.C., think tank
that's attached to a university. Jackie was the director
of the Center for Women there, and I'd been referred to
her by my friend April. Jackie was just some random
woman, as far as I was concerned. Later, I found out
that April had deliberately set out to work for Jackie
herself. April really wanted Jackie to be her mentor. But
after April came to work for Jackie, she experienced this
big disillusionment with her, and she found out that
Jackie really wasn't who she thought she was going to
be for her. She found Jackie to be kind of harsh and
critical and not very supportive. April had her bubble
burst almost immediately.*

*On the other hand, I didn't have any
expectations about Jackie whatsoever. I mean, she
was just a co-worker, as far as I was concerned. And
I thought, if we get along, great, you know? And it
turned out that we had this slowly evolving relationship
where she really, really grew to respect me, and I really,
really grew to respect her.*

Like Charlotte, Tyler found her mentor among her co-workers in an office where she worked during her late twenties:

I was instantly attracted to my mentor, who looked really well put together. She's in her late fifties, she looked like she had a little cash, and, you know, she just looked like she was big and tall. I've always been drawn to tall people. She wore shoulder pads and looked powerful. There was an immediate spark of interest between us. We really liked each other, and she just took me under her wing. She just decided I was valuable. It was the one relationship—unlike my relationship with my mother—where I didn't feel like I had to be really attentive to her and make sure that she was okay. It felt like this kind of nurturing connection where it was enough for her to just focus on me.

When I first met her, I was really depressed. I had recently gotten married, but I just felt confused about a lot of things. And I couldn't understand why I was depressed and confused. She's really direct with me and asks thought-provoking questions. She helped me figure out a lot of the practical things that at the time just seemed beyond anything I could figure out by myself.

Over the last four years, it's become obvious to me that I'm making more and more progress in my life, and I think that it has a lot to do with the way Janet believes in me and makes me feel like I'm valuable.

It's interesting to note that in none of these situations did any of the women consciously set out to find a mentor. In Charlotte's story, her friend April was only disappointed when she deliberately set out to make a mentor out of Jackie, who eventually became Charlotte's mentor instead. Tyler recognized her mentor right away; but, for Charlotte, the relationship was a slow brew.

A mentor can suddenly appear on your horizon, although she may not meet your preconceptions about what a fairy godmother should look like. Leah told me her first impression of Mabel, the British Quaker who sponsored the then fourteen-year-old Leah's escape from Nazi Germany:

> *She was really a rather—I'd have to call her an ugly woman to look at. That was just my impression when I realized that she was the one who was going to be my guardian, there among all the other people in the waiting room at the railroad station. You know, now I think of her as sort of a saint. But at the time I wasn't terribly impressed.*

When, in her forties, Page decided to start her own business, she located someone in her industry she wanted to emulate:

> *I asked her to be my mentor. I just said, "Would you help me with my business? I see that you do it very well." I wasn't anybody or anything, but I guess because I asked her, she was happy to help me be successful. She was just this delightful woman who saw potential in me.*
>
> *I was experienced enough to know that in order to be successful, I would need other people's help. So I created this board of advisors, and she and a couple of other women were on it, and we went through the machinations of trying to create this thing that had never*

been created before. Maybe she saw that I was this goal-oriented person, and that reminded her of herself. I don't know. People aren't always that generous. But she was feeding me with information and ideas, and she'd send me to conferences and things. She'd say, "You need to meet this person or see that person's operation." It was pretty great, because I got just what I asked for.

Hope was also in her forties when she met her mentor. Like Tyler and Page, she felt an instant bond: "I just knew, I just loved her. It was absolutely wonderful to have someone with whom I could, in safety, talk about my ideas."

Where you are in your life will probably have a lot to do with how you make your connection with a mentor. Betsy told me, "I think one of the things that comes in your working life is that gradually you get a much better idea of what's right for you and what isn't—what kinds of choices that you want to make. Like a lot of people, I decided to change career direction when I was in my thirties. I was already launched on that path when I met the woman who became my mentor for this new phase of my career, and who affected me in so many other ways as well."

Lori is a thirty-something junior high school teacher who says she just lucked out in finding her mentor:

She was chairperson of my department. I was the only beginning teacher that year, and we were just two doors down the hall from each other. So part of it was just coincidence, and part of it was that I think she felt a little bit like she owed me something, too. She told me, when they hired me at the end of June, what I was going to be teaching. Then something happened, and they had to change the curriculum two days before the year started. She was just the messenger, but I think she felt pretty awful about it. Here I was teaching my first class and I hadn't read seven out of the nine books I was supposed to teach! So I think she felt somewhat obligated to help me.

As Cathy pointed out, sometimes we find mentors in women who closely resemble our hopes about the sort of person we'll be in the future. This was the case for Violetta:

When I graduated from college, I was doing work for a very successful math program for high school students and undergraduates. One of the goals of the program was to identify students who were traditionally underrepresented in math and science. While I was there, I met a high school teacher who was on sabbatical and who came to look at these programs. She actually remembered me from when I was eighteen years old and taking these math classes at the university, where she'd come in to watch. And so she remembered me, but I didn't remember her.

Besides her work as a high school teacher, she was also doing a lot of professional development with teachers. So, four years later, when she needed an evaluator for this program, she thought of me. That's how we got connected.

I had started to seriously think about a career in math teaching. We talked a lot about the curriculum, the kind of work she was doing with teachers, and I realized that I was learning a lot just from how she talked with her colleagues, and from absorbing her values. Her teaching philosophy, and the students she was trying to serve, reflected my own interests.

She has a similar background to mine. She's very politically active. She's Latina, like I am, and she has a really strong sense of social justice and how education is a part of that. And math education was her specialty. So when it came time for me to start considering graduate school, she and I went to lunch one day, and I asked her what she thought. I had asked other people, but I was particularly interested in what she had to say. The conversation we had that day really helped determine what I wound up doing. And it's a conversation that's been ongoing now for the past six years.

In real life, as opposed to fairy tales, our mentors don't usually appear on the horizon in a magic bubble or in a shower of glowing lights. We may not even know until many years following our first encounter that she has become a mentor to us. There is sometimes an immediate sense of recognition; but sometimes the knowledge dawns only slowly, even over a period of many years.

But there does seem to be an element of fate in all these stories—a sense in which that first encounter seems, in retrospect, to have somehow been inevitable. The writer and critic Yi-Tsi Mei Feuerwerker said, "I have come to believe that I have been fated, 'chosen' even ... to study Ding Ling the writer. Certainly my choice of subject and the events that resulted have profoundly changed my life. They have not only determined what I was to do and how I was to spend my time, but they have also affected my ways of thinking about myself" (16).

Joyce, a writer, said:

I got to know my mentor in a pretty roundabout way. I'd written a review of one of her books of short stories; she wrote me a letter because she liked my review. I wrote her a long, heartfelt letter in return, telling her how much I admired her. A full year passed, and I felt stupid for having gushed the way I had. Then a letter arrived from her with apologies because she'd been ill—and an invitation to come visit her.

In a lot of ways, that first day when I walked up to her door with an enormous bouquet of flowers, I felt like my whole life had been leading up to that moment. I knew that my life as a writer, as I'd known it up till then, was about to change.

2

Mentoring and Mothering

I don't think a mentor—or anyone else, really— can tell you what you want to do with your life or what you love best. All a mentor can do—and this is a big "all"—is help you get back in touch with that part of yourself that has known all along.
—Joyce

I was doing all the right things with my mentor, which a daughter often cannot do. Her real daughter wasn't able to do this with her, and I could never have that kind of relationship with my own mother. To my mind, my mother was doing everything wrong.
—Simone

I think especially if we've gone through life feeling a little bit destroyed by our mothers, it can be a healing experience to find an older woman who has power over you who will not destroy you, but will do the opposite; who will nurture you through this passage in some way.

—Cathy

Taking the "Men" Out of Mentors

It may come as a surprise to some that the very first official mentor was female. The word was first used in Homer's *Odyssey* as the name of Odysseus's trusted friend left in charge of the household when Odysseus sets off on his epic journey. But it's actually the goddess Athena, disguised as Mentor, who serves as guide to Odysseus's son Telemachus in his search for his father. The dictionary tells us that the word "mentor" probably meant "advisor" in ancient Greek, and comes from the Indo-European root *men—*, meaning "to think." This is consonant with the common view that our women mentors are rather goddess-like people who guide us by causing us to think about things—most notably ourselves—in new ways.

Among the women I interviewed, there were some who described a great relationship with a mother who met all their emotional needs head-on. What was fascinating was that these same women almost all identified their mother as their mentor. The one exception was Violetta: "I will say that my mother has had a profound influence on my life. But I actually don't think of her as my mentor. I think of her as my mother."

But the distinction between good mothering and good mentoring was not at all so clear for the other people I spoke to who felt adequately nurtured by their mothers. Some of these women found another woman to mentor them after their mother died. But for each of them, Mom was the first mentor and role model, a well-spring to which they returned again and again for strength, wisdom, and encouragement.

Jordan's mother successfully raised thirteen children and was a pioneer in her work, as well as a pillar of the community. She was so very competent, powerful, and almost saintlike in her capacity to give encouragement and love that it was difficult for Jordan, even as an adult, to step out of the role of her mother's child. Jordan explained, "I felt I was a young girl all the way until my mom passed. I did not grow up until after my mom was gone."

After Kirin graduated from business school and got her first corporate job, she was taken under the wing of a slightly older female colleague who gave her much the same kind of encouragement and guidance Kirin's mother had given her as a child, but in the context of the adult world:

> *Just seeing the way my mentor was at work, and the way she handled herself in difficult situations, was sometimes enough to give me the clue I needed to solve my own problem and get on with things. In that regard, she was a lot like my mom—even though my mom would have been at sea in a high-powered corporate environment. They're completely different as women; they move in completely different worlds. But both had lessons to teach me about listening to myself, knowing what I want to do and then going after it single-mindedly, with one hundred percent commitment, trust in myself, and a great attitude.*

Mentors as Mothers

When we talk about our female mentors, we tend to use words that are powerfully evocative of an idealized mother-daughter relationship. Our mentor validates our identity, potential, and ambitions by giving the gifts that are given by an effective parent to her child. We feel listened to, understood, and valued by our mentor in a way that frees us to be ourselves and pursue our most cherished goals.

One of the most fascinating patterns that emerged from the interviews was that many of the women whose mentors weren't a blood relative felt they'd been inadequately mothered the first time around. These experiences ranged the gamut from truly negligent mothers to mothers who were no doubt conscientious, but simply didn't fit that particular child's emotional, spiritual, or intellectual needs.

Tyler, who runs a talent agency, warned that her story was laughably transparent: her mother and her mentor share the same first name. Tyler is thirty now, successful in her career, and happily married with a baby son she dotes on. She believes that her mentor fulfilled the role of "the good mom" in contrast to her biological mother, who always seemed to do everything wrong:

> *My mom was a big drug addict, alcoholic—you know, a fuck-up, basically. She just blew it in every possible way—several divorces and incidences of near-homelessness and a lot of other really bad stuff. I've always felt that there was a right way to do things, but my mom just didn't know what they were. And so I think I've spent my whole life looking for someone who did—who will show me how to do things like set a table. Do you know what I'm saying?*

Many of us can identify with what Tyler was saying. There are so many things we learn about, sometimes painfully, as adults that we wish we'd been taught as children.

Some of these things are questions of courtesy; some touch upon more basic issues of honor or responsibility.

Joyce's experience had some similarities to Tyler's:

> *There were all sorts of things I grew up not questioning—like whether it was okay to swipe towels from hotel rooms, or stiff someone on a tip. My grandparents were from the old country, Depression-era school of thinking, and they passed that on to my parents, who passed it on to me. Saving money or getting something for free was sometimes more important than doing what was right. It took me years of shocked looks from my friends before I realized there might be something wrong with that way of looking at things— at least for someone in my era and in my economic situation. There were other lessons I wish I'd learned earlier, too—like sticking with things even if they're hard for me, and taking my promises seriously.*

Some people never get over the deficits from their childhood. Others are able to put these deficits to work as powerful incentives to find another way. Tyler's success in her career, as well as her devotion as a mother, have been fueled by the negative lessons from her earliest years. The chaos of her childhood fed her desire to build up a by-the-books, beautifully organized business, and to provide the close contact and consistency for her son that Tyler never got from her mother. She told me, "I've always been really interested in etiquette and rules. I like rules. I want people to tell me what to do and how to do it. I really like order and structure, because I didn't have any of that when I was growing up."

Tyler's words echo those of memoirist and novelist Jane Lazarre. In her essay "Charlotte's Web: Reading *Jane Eyre* Over Time," Lazarre wrote: "I too was always on the lookout for a mother, continually choosing new women to use in my effort to create a fully imagined maternal presence in my head ... who would like me, notice my goodness ... from whom I might learn the simple things a 'woman does.' As the daughter of a powerful father, I was sure I was human, but being a woman was something I had to learn" (227).

Lazarre writes of her own mentor, "The aspect of her character that drew me into a spiral of ecstatic copying was the graceful way she had of ordering the physical world ... I set about to do things the way she did until her patterns had become my own" (227).

At the other end of the scale from Tyler's chaotic childhood is Iris, an art school graduate who works as a pattern-maker for a San Francisco couturier. Iris describes her upbringing as run-of-the-mill suburban:

> *My mom was not very learned or accomplished and had very little ambition. When I was growing up, I couldn't see what good she'd done with her life and didn't particularly admire what she'd made of her life.*
> *I didn't want to be who she was or follow in her path. I didn't want to be in a marriage with a man who was brighter and told you so all the time. You know? I wanted to be able to stand on my own.*
>
> *My mentors were the ones who showed me how to do that. They were really different from my mom. And though I loved my mom and got a lot of nurturing from*

her on one level, I didn't get direction as far as how to make a life of my own.

It seems that we not only need a mom, but the right mom—and the search can take us well beyond childhood. In *Woman: An Intimate Geography,* Natalie Angier writes: "We keep looking for our mothers and those mythical creatures our female mentors . . ." (236). But both quests—the search for our mothers and the search for our mentors—are variations on the oldest quest in the world, our search for our own identities. The ideal of the perfect mother figure holds that there is someone out there in the world who will be able to allay our anxiety by telling us exactly who we are and what we need to do with our lives.

In her essay "Daughters Writing: Toward a Theory of Women's Biography," literary critic Bell Gale Chevigny discusses a similar dynamic that occurs when women biographers write about other women in history. She says that there's a stage in the biographical process when author and subject become "surrogate mothers" to each other. Unlike the fantasy of the perfect mother, the fantasy of the surrogate mother describes a reciprocal relationship. Both women in the process—in Chevigny's paradigm, both the biographer and her subject—are engaged in a struggle to fully achieve their respective identities. "Both nurture not an infant, but a girl or woman; and for both, nurture is a sanctioning of their autonomy" (373).

If our mother cannot or will not help us solve the riddle of our identity, we may look for a female mentor to do the job. Joyce said:

*I truly believe that each of is born knowing exactly who
we are. And then childhood has a way of beating the
knowledge out of us, or at least confusing us so much
that we may spend much of our adult lives trying
painfully, over the course of many years, to remember.
But I think it has that quality whenever someone has a
great moment of insight about what they really want to
do with their lives; when they discover a vocation. It's
like, "Oh, yeah! Now I remember. This is what I've
always loved." I don't think a mentor—or anyone else,
really—can tell you what you want to do with your life
or what you love best. All a mentor can do—and this
is a big "all"—is help you get back in touch with that
part of yourself that has known all along.*

Love You, Hate You

How many children grow up with the feeling of having
simply been born into the wrong family? If there is no
same-sex role model at home that can comprehend and
validate a girl's hopes and dreams, she may not get the
developmental boost she needs there. In leaving home to
find a mentor, a young woman is not necessarily looking
for a substitute mother, but for someone who can nurture
her adult self and be midwife to her identity as a full-
fledged individual in the adult world.

This was true for Simone, whose parents were too
busy coping with the stresses of everyday survival to really
pay attention to what she was doing. At the age of twenty,
Simone saved up enough money to travel to the United

States, where she thought she would at least have the chance of creating a different destiny for herself.

Simone knew that she had the ability to get an education, but it took someone from the outside who had faith in her before she could allow herself to be successful. She told me that she was like a surrogate daughter to her first mentor, in that Simone was really able to listen to her mentor's encouragement and act upon it: "I was doing all the right things with my mentor, which a daughter often cannot do. Her real daughter wasn't able to do this with her, and I could never have that kind of relationship with my own mother. To my mind, my mother was doing everything wrong."

Many of us may recognize Simone's critical stance toward her mother. Natalie Angier writes:

> *I've often noticed that daughters are hard on their mothers, much harder than sons are. Women will romanticize their fathers and forgive them many sins and failings, but toward their mothers they show no mercy. Whatever the mother did, she could do no right. The mother was cold and negligent, the mother was overbearing and smothering, the mother was timid, the mother was a shrew. Even feminism did not cure us of our mother hatred, our mother flu. We cling to our anger at our mothers. We don't want to give it up. (233–34)*

In their book *The Reproduction of Mothering: Psychoanalysis and the Sociology of Gender*, social scientists Nancy Chodorow and Susan Contratto suggest that we harbor a belief in our mothers as—in potential, at least—"all-powerful" beings.

The offshoot of this is that, on the one hand, we blame our mothers for not living up to this perfect image. But, on the other hand, we hold tight to the fantasy that our mothers can somehow *become* perfect.

Research psychologist Paula J. Caplan discusses this unrealistic expectation of mothers and its consequences in her book *Don't Blame Mother: Mending the Mother-Daughter Relationship*: "Mothers are either idealized or blamed for everything that goes wrong" (2).

Caryn talked about how her expectations of her mother complicated their relationship:

> *Even though my dad was clearly the bad guy in my family, and we were all terrified of him, it was my mother I continued to blame and be angry at throughout much of my adult life, on into my forties. Somehow, even the fact that he was so rotten was* her *fault. If she'd been smarter or stronger or more assertive or just hadn't ever married him in the first place, we would have been spared any amount of suffering and pain. Looking back now, it just seems so irrational to me that I felt that way.*

As the mother of a daughter, it's very hard to win. Natalie Angier writes:

> *I've gone through long stretches of hating my mother mindlessly and obsessively, of crying bitterly when I think of her, of writing small fables in which she is the Ogress, the Great Gaping Cardiophage with no heart of her own. But then there are other times when I stop myself in the middle of a mother fit and say, This isn't rational, it isn't fair, and it's a bad precedent. Think*

now how you might drag yourself out of the sewer of
mother hatred, lest your daughter grow up and blast you
with hate and blame of her own. (233–34)

There are developmental reasons for our anger against our mothers where no parallel reasons exist for us to reject our fathers. Some form of rejection or rebellion seems to almost always be necessary to allow a woman to sort out where her mother ends and she herself begins. Bell Gale Chevigny writes: "Female autonomy cannot be experienced without a sense of abandoning the mother" (373).

Never going through this period of rebellion can make it hard for a woman to step fully into her adult identity while her mother is still alive. Jordan told me:

My mother was definitely my mentor. I couldn't believe
how she got done everything she got done. She was like
a miracle every day of the week. But the truth is, I
continued thinking of my life in terms of what I would
be when I grew up long after I had supposedly become
a grown- up—in fact, long after I'd married, had kids,
and gone through a divorce. It wasn't until after Mama
passed that I started thinking about how in the world
I was going to fill those shoes.

Bridget, a dancer and dance teacher, had a similar story. "My mother just also happened to be my mentor. There were no other females who took me on or took an active interest in me, and there was nobody that I felt that profound connection with; so maybe for me those boundaries are blurred."

Because their love is at least supposed to be unconditional, mothers are often faced with a credibility problem.

Their compliments to their daughters may fall on deaf ears if the child's basic sense of self-worth is at all shaky. A mentor who isn't a blood relation tends to be easier to listen to and believe. This was true for Stephanie, who left a doctoral program to pursue a career in filmmaking:

When I look back, I can see that my mother tried in her own way to give me the encouragement I needed to pursue my goals. But I think I tended to discount whatever encouraging things she said, because—well, it was her job to encourage me. Of course she was going to encourage me. She was my mom. When some of the very same things came out of my mentor's mouth, though, I could really hear them for the first time. She wasn't under any obligation to think well of me—and so what she said seemed more believable, somehow. I figured she must really mean what she was saying, and it made it seem more like the truth.

As much as a mother's compliments may fall on deaf ears, her criticisms of her daughter may cut deep and true, often leaving terrible scars. Maria, a physician, said:

No matter what I accomplished in terms of my career, my mother has always let me know through the subtlest means—little sighs, longing looks at her friends' grandchildren, little comments that she probably thinks are completely innocuous—how much more she would have liked it if I'd simply dropped out of school at the age of sixteen or so and started having babies. Not only did I defy convention by staying in school for what seemed like forever to her; but I also chose not to marry or have children, and I live with my female partner.

> *As proud as I am of myself for what I've done with my life, there will always be a little hole torn inside me by that lack of my mother's approval. I think there's a part of all of us that longs for that maternal approval more than anything else in the world—and it hurts, on some level, to know that no matter what you do, what you accomplish, you're never going to earn it.*

It's striking that these criticisms never seem to lose their power, even if the daughter is herself a grandmother. Kate, who is in her mid-sixties, told me that speaking with her mother on the telephone is still something she has to brace herself for. She has developed a little meditation she does beforehand, reassuring herself that she is a valuable person, worthy of being loved: "And then, when I'm talking with her, and she's going on and on about herself and never asks me about myself, and is completely uninterested in whatever is going on in my life or my children's lives, I keep repeating inside my head, 'I am lovable. I am worthy.' I just let her words blow by me, and I wait until the phone call is over."

A female mentor can provide a woman with a way to satisfy the needs her own mother wasn't able to fulfill. And in doing this, the mentor can serve as a catalyst for healing old wounds between daughters and their mothers. Marcella talked about how her mentor affected her relationship with her mother:

> *It wasn't at all a conscious process and, at the time, I would have said that my relationship with my mentor had absolutely nothing to do with my relationship with my mom—which had always been difficult, from as far*

back as I can remember. But with the benefit of hindsight, I can see that the one bond flourishing helped the other bond to heal. No doubt, there was something inside me *that changed, which made it possible for me to relate to my mom in a new way. I was suddenly able to be more generous emotionally. And it was only when* I *changed that she was able to change. I think my mother and I might have been caught in lockstep together, doing the same dance for the rest of our lives, if I hadn't gotten that infusion of encouragement and kindness from my mentor.*

Healing the Mother-Daughter Bond

Good mothering is an art. Giving birth is no guarantee of being or becoming an adept practitioner of this art. There seem to be two distinct and very different veins that can be mined for mothering skills. One is the precedent of having had a good mother oneself. The other, perhaps surprisingly, is having had a rather bad mother. A determined woman given to thinking hard about the reasons why things happen can use her own painful experience as a negative model from which she can differentiate her own mothering. In this sense, even bad mothers can serve as mentors—although, in this case, it would be more accurate to call them "antimentors."

Tyler told me about the very different ways in which her mother and her mentor reacted to the launching of Tyler's business:

We'd signed all the papers, and we were about to have a party. This was a huge step for me, and everything pointed to it being a really great move—the lawyers, everyone thought I was going to make some big bucks. I got off the phone with my mom, who was really upset because she couldn't make it to the party. She had something else she'd scheduled, and she couldn't get out of it. She knew she'd blown it, but she was acting like it was no big deal, trying to rationalize the whole thing. I got off the phone with her, and I felt like, it's just never enough, no matter what I do. I put together this business, for God's sake, you know? It's not enough just to be successful.

I was obsessing about this when the doorbell rang. There was a huge bouquet of flowers from the other Janet, with this beautiful note that said, "Congratulations on your coups, *my dear! I'm really proud of you. I can't make it tonight. I'm sorry. But here you go." I really appreciated that gesture because I felt like, oh, that's the appropriate way to handle something like this. And there it was in a nutshell, the bad and the good. The right response and the wrong one.*

A woman whose emotional needs were not met by her own mother may well have a hard time providing what her daughter needs, especially if she hasn't recognized and dealt with these issues. The good news is that frustrated mother-daughter relationships are fertile ground for the production both of willing mentors and receptive protégées. Terry said, "It heartens me, this idea that there are second chances to get your needs fulfilled, in terms of things your family of origin didn't provide—that you can heal your relationship with your parents in a relationship with a mentor."

Our female mentors open doors for us, inspire us, and push us to succeed. But their gifts to us that we most cherish are those that reflect the tenderness of a mother's love. This seems to be true no matter what age we are or in what awe we hold our mentors. In her essay "Hannah Arendt: Thinking as We Are," feminist philosopher Elizabeth Kamarck Minnich wrote of her academic mentor, "She had no qualms about playing a caretaking role when it expressed real care and not a role. She fed me, she worried about whether my coat was warm enough" (183).

Lori was brought up in California by a mother who flitted from one New Age guru to another, much to the detriment of her family's stability. Lori's mom was grappling with her own developmental issues at the very time when her daughter needed a strong and consistent role model. Lori talked about how her mentors have helped fulfill her unmet needs:

> *The woman who has been my mentor most recently has a teenage daughter she's been having a lot of problems with, and we joke about it, because she was going through some pretty hardcore stuff with her daughter, and I was going through some pretty hardcore stuff with my mom. We joked about the fact that we were going to play mother-daughter for a while.*
>
> *Those relationships with my mentors are absolutely what has taken me down the path that I went down. My relationship with my parents was so lacking when I needed them most that having other people sort of parent me in various ways is the only thing that got me*

*here. My current mentor and I are putting the finishing
touches on a manuscript about a whole new approach
to teaching reading at the secondary level, and I'm going
back to school to get my Master's degree based on this
work. She mothered me through my first year of teaching
in an urban setting, during which one particular class
was the bane of my existence and sent me home crying
a lot of the time.*

Paula talked about the irony of seeking a mentor to
meet her unmet needs, while her mother was simultane-
ously mentoring and nurturing others:

*When I was in my twenties and even my thirties, it
used to drive me nuts when women close to my own age
would confide in me about my mother's wonderfully
nurturing behavior toward them. My first internal
reaction was that these women simply didn't know what
they were talking about. My mother, who (I have come
to understand) is quite a wonderful woman, had always
been a minimalist in the nurture department—and I spent
my childhood and many years thereafter feeling angry and
resentful about this. The more I expressed my disappointment, though, the more my mother kept me at arm's length.*

*It took me a long time to comprehend that her
experience of mothering me was just as painful and
exasperating for her as my experience of being the
daughter who was always longing for more than my
mother felt comfortable giving. It was a bummer for her
to be around me, even long after I had supposedly grown
up. I always made her feel guilty and inadequate—
hardly a pleasant combination.*

> *With my much younger sister, and with other informally adopted daughters, my mother had a much happier, more satisfying experience. What I failed to see, there from the outskirts of what I saw as my mother's loving circle, was that the very frustrations of our relationship were probably what inspired her to listen more attentively and give of herself more unstintingly to others.*

The psychologist Daphne Rose Kingma, in *Coming Apart,* writes about how our love relationships often serve the purpose of helping us complete developmental tasks that we were unable to complete in childhood for one reason or another. Perhaps the same holds true for mentor-protégée relationships, and on both sides. Mothers such as Paula's can find satisfactions in being a mentor that may have eluded them in their experience of mothering a daughter. And daughters who did not get what they wanted from their own mother can complete some of their work of growing fully into adulthood through their relationship with a female mentor.

Cathy, a paralegal, said, "I think especially if we've gone through life feeling a little bit destroyed by our mothers, it can be a healing experience to find an older woman who has power over you who will not destroy you, but will do the opposite; who will nurture you through this passage in some way."

Simone talked about how her relationship with her mentor actually healed her relationship with her mother:

> *My second mentor helped me see what my mother had gone through. I was finally able to forgive my mother for many things she said, because I was finally able to see*

what she had gone through in her life. And so my
mentor was able to open doors for me that I had closed
for myself. She made me realize that I had a lot to
talk about concerning my mother. And now, in fact,
I have a good relationship with my mother.

Tyler, whose experience was similar to Simone's, put it well: "Once you get your needs met, then you don't have to be pummeling someone, begging them to meet your needs when they can't, when they're incapable. In a way, your mentor does your mother a great favor. I know that, for me, it's made a lot of forgiveness possible that I think wouldn't have been possible otherwise, if that place inside me had remained unfilled."

Lori's mother recognized how important Lori's mentor had been in her daughter's life. Lori said:

My mom specifically asked me if I'd get her together
with my mentor, Christine, so that she could thank
Christine for everything she did for me. Christine is a
dyed-in-the-wool New Yorker and thinks my mom is
kind of a crazy Californian. But I think she was
moved by my mom saying that. And because of
Christine, my relationship with my mom has really
gotten a lot better.

Surrender

For Kate, a sixty-three-year-old artist, reparenting issues are not just a symbolic part of the mentor-protégée relationship. She is also proof positive that mentors do not necessarily have to be older than their protégées. Kate met someone who could fill the "empty place inside her" at a twelve-step meeting, someone who was very upbeat and had, according to Kate, a strong spiritual base. Kate's sponsor agreed to talk to her for half an hour, three times a week, at seven-thirty in the morning. Kate described their relationship:

> *My mentor is in her late forties. She's not young enough to be my daughter, but she's never had a child, and she chose never to have children. So she has adopted me and I have adopted her. She says she feels like I was sent for her—without the diapers and all that stuff she never wanted to do. About four years ago, I went into therapy to try to heal some of the pain I was feeling about everything my mother never gave me. And the therapist said, "Before we do this work, you're going to need to find a substitute mother. You basically have an orphan script, even though you weren't an orphan. There was no one there for you, ever."*
>
> *There's a sense of surrender as I listen to my mentor. I allow her to mother me. I go into a state when she's telling me about some spiritual truth and I say to myself, "Get quiet now and listen to a voice that would have been so wonderful to hear when you were so young and needed to hear these things." I never had any guidance about how to live life, what life's about, or why we're here. So I just surrender and I listen, and I talk about whatever it is that's troubling me at the time.*

Kate's story is echoed in writer Jane Lazarre's analysis of character development in Charlotte Bronte's nineteenth-century novel, *Jane Eyre.* Lazarre writes, "At several crucial points in the novel, Jane looks around for mothers to adopt. In a sense she is looking for lessons in how to be a woman because that identification, which ought to be effortless, has by necessity of her loss [Jane Eyre is an orphan] become a conscious lack in her" (226).

It shouldn't be all that surprising that there's a maternal element in the mentor-protégée relationship. All the words we have to describe this relationship—from protégée ("one who is protected") to the title of this book—are evocative of the mother-child bond.

This is not to say that mothers of grown daughters who have gone out and sought female mentors need to fault themselves for having mothered inadequately; nor that grown women under the protection of a female mentor, or in search of one, should feel less than whole or healthy because of their need. Jordan explained:

> *No one could have a better mentor or a better role model than I had in my mother. But after she passed, and after I got over my anger at her leaving me, I realized there was another kind of mentor I needed—someone who would give me a hand as I jumped over that fence into the next part of my life, that part where I'm not thinking about myself as a daughter or a baby sister, but as a grown-up woman who can accomplish things in her own right. As a woman who has something important to contribute to the world, all on her own.*

The Evolutionary Roots of the Mentor-Protégée Relationship

Anthropologist Jared Diamond makes a strong case for menopause as an evolutionary survival strategy, rather than as a mere symptom of our attenuated life spans and worn-out reproductive systems. He wrote in *Discover* magazine that older women who are not able to bear children are necessary to the well-being and survival of the tribe in traditional hunter-gatherer societies.

Diamond builds on earlier work by anthropologists Kristen Hawkes, James O'Connell, and Nicholas Blurton Jones, who studied foraging by women of different ages among the Hadza hunter-gatherers of Tanzania. These scholars found that the postmenopausal women of the tribe worked far longer hours than the younger women at gathering food, and were far more efficient in their methods (because, presumably, they knew more about edible wild plants and where to find them).

The logical extension of these observations is that our human ancestors recognized the evolutionary advantage of having postmenopausal women around. Not being tied down by the demands of nursing and rearing young children, these older women could gather food and medicinal herbs for the others. Diamond writes, "They also act as baby-sitters for grandchildren, thereby helping their adult children churn out more babies bearing Grandma's genes. . . . We moderns . . . find it impossible to conceive of the overwhelming importance of elderly people in preliterate societies as repositories of information and experience" (130).

In traditional societies, there is a symbiotic, nurturing relationship between these two categories of women. Since everyone in a small tribe is pretty much related to everyone else, the bond can jump beyond the mother-daughter-grandchild connection and still serve the needs of natural selection. The older woman's knowledge and experience can mean the difference between a tribe's survival and its destruction in the face of a natural disaster.

An example of this is the cyclone in 1910 that hit Rennell Island, one of the Solomon Islands, blowing down most of the forest, destroying people's gardens, and driving the islanders to the brink of starvation. Diamond writes, "Islanders survived by eating fruits of wild plant species that were normally not eaten. But doing so required detailed knowledge about which plants are poisonous, which are not poisonous, and whether and how the poison can be removed by some technique of food preparation" (131). It was the old women of the island, the most experienced food gatherers, who were in possession of this information and thus were able to save the tribe from perishing.

Our modern-day version of the mentor-protégée relationship appears to be an outgrowth of this evolutionary bargain between younger and older women—even though it has nothing directly to do, at this point in our history, with gathering food. Many of the women I interviewed, however, said that their mentor helped them launch their career—allowing them to win bread, if not to gather it. Marcella said:

> *My primary professional mentor, herself a famous journalist, memoirist, and political activist, helped me greatly expand my writing career from the narrow confines in which I had, up to that time, contained it. And by doing that, she also expanded my possibilities for earning a living by my pen. So much of what I used to think of as my refusal to sell out had much more to do with a kind of rigidity and a fear, really, about being successful. She loved every minute of her success,*

and she gave a hundred percent of her mind and heart
to every sentence she ever committed to paper. If that's
selling out, well, then I want to sell out, too!

Survival, these days, is a much different affair than it
was when we were all hunter-gatherers living from handful
to handful of food. But we are as much in need of a leg up
in our quest for satisfactions having nothing to do with
food or immediate survival as our ancestors were as they
scoured the land for things to eat.

In *Woman: An Intimate Geography*, Natalie Angier writes
that "a woman's mother-lust, her need for the older female
and for other women generally, is ... ancient" (236).

The good offices of a well-meaning older woman
experienced in the ways of survival can mean the difference
now—as it did then—between a happy life and a frustrated
one. It really doesn't matter all that much if that woman is
the very one who carried you in her belly. In the sense that
one generation gives birth to the next one, every older
woman is mother—and a potential mentor—to every
younger one. Kate's story would have us draw the even
more general conclusion that every woman is a potential
mother and mentor to every woman in her orbit, no matter
what the ages of the women involved.

Maria talked about the ways in which the mentor-
protégée bond can heal old wounds:

The more I learn about life, the more I've come to believe
that our purpose is to make ourselves as whole and
healed as possible—to gather all the pieces of the puzzle
together and put them in place, until we are finally,
completely, ourselves. If a female mentor can help us with

this task, certainly it's cause for celebration rather than accusatory finger-pointing, either at our mothers or ourselves. The really good part is that even if the mother-daughter relationship doesn't work as well as it might the first time around, you both get a second chance.

3

Magic Mirrors

You're at a crossroads, and there's either an opportunity or a crisis. That time when my mentor helped me so much was a sensitive period in my life, a critical point in time when the relationship allowed certain things to gel for me and had a profound influence on the direction my life has taken.

—Violetta

When Adele looked at me, she saw the girl she once was. And when I looked at her, I saw the woman I wanted to become.

—Ally

At first I worried that I was taking too much in my relationship with my mentor. I couldn't imagine what I would possibly have to offer her in return for all her help. When I blurted this out to her one day, when we were taking one of our power walks together around the lake at lunchtime, she stopped dead in her tracks and told me not to ever worry about what I was giving her, because she felt that the relationship helped her every bit as much as it helps me.

—Kirin

Mentors as Mirrors

"Snow White" is, in a sense, the quintessential antimentor story. The wicked queen, who is well-positioned to guide and nurture her step-daughter, instead does everything in her power to engineer Snow White's demise. Jealousy is the driving force behind the queen's malevolence; and the queen's magic mirror is the goad to her rancor.

Both the queen and Snow White are great beauties. But whereas the queen is nearing the end of her run—presumably, she's somewhere in middle age, probably around thirty, given the shorter life spans in the days when fairytales were spawned—Snow White is in the first bloom of youth. A prized possession, the mirror has been in the habit of telling the queen exactly what she wants to hear: to wit, that she is fairest in the land.

But the mirror is a truth-teller rather than a flatterer. When Snow White ceases to be a child and becomes an object of desire, the mirror confirms the queen's worst fear, that she will have to cede her place as "fairest in the land" to the younger woman. The queen can see no way around this nasty turn of events except to get rid of Snow White, which she takes every pain to do.

In his classic work, *The Uses of Enchantment,* Bruno Bettelheim gives us a look at various fairy tales—including "Snow White"—through a psychoanalytical lens: "In a girl's oedipal fantasy, the mother is split into two figures: the pre-oedipal wonderful good mother and the oedipal evil stepmother. The good mother, so the fantasy goes, would never have been jealous of her daughter or have prevented the prince (father) and the girl from living happily together. So for the oedipal girl, belief and trust in the goodness of the pre-oedipal mother, and deep loyalty to her, tend to reduce the guilt about what the girl wishes would happen to the (step)mother who stands in her way" (114).

The mentor-protégée relationship is a second chance to play out the mother-daughter relationship in the absence of oedipal conflicts. In other words, there is usually no father figure or lover—no "prince"—for whose attentions the mentor and the protégée are competing; there is no "split" necessary between the good mother and the wicked mother substitute. The mentor gets to play the role of the fairy godmother who helps the protégée resolve her conflicts and progress to the next stage in her development as an individual.

The mentor serves her protégée as a benevolent version of the magic mirror in "Snow White." In looking at her mentor, the protégée sees a vision of the future, and a possible version of herself, that pleases her. As long as the mentor provides this mirroring, the protégée feels empowered to carry on in pursuit of her most deeply cherished goals.

According to the psychiatrist Heinz Kohut, author of *The Analysis of the Self: A Systematic Approach to the Psychoanalytic Treatment of Narcissistic Personality Disorder* and other classic texts on psychoanalysis, mirroring is a crucial stage in a young child's development. From infancy on, our same-sex parent is an editorializing mirror to our hopes and fears. By looking at our mothers and registering their reactions to us, we get our first lessons about our identity, strengths, weaknesses, and potential.

A woman's attachment to mirrors as a gauge of her identity and progress extends well beyond childhood. Whether or not we have been effectively "mirrored" by our mothers, our need for externalized self-reflection reasserts itself through the different stages of our lives, from infancy through old age. "Who am I?" and "What is possible for me?" are questions we continue to ask ourselves throughout our lives. We often find new answers to these questions in the presence or under the influence of a female mentor.

Like a fairy godmother, our mentor usually makes her first appearance at a critical juncture in our life. Her role as helper is by definition a transitory one. Violetta's academic mentor showed up when she was at a crucial crossroads in her academic career, unsure of which way to go:

> *I don't feel it as a mentoring relationship now in the same way as I felt it twelve, thirteen years ago. And that makes me wonder if thinking of a person as a mentor has something to do with the stage of your own life—a kind of sphere of influence that somebody has at a time when you're vulnerable or where you need something. You're at a crossroads, and there's either an opportunity or a crisis. That time when my mentor helped me so much was a sensitive period in my life, a critical point in time when the relationship allowed certain things to gel for me and had a profound influence on the direction my life has taken. I would define that opportunity for what I think of as mentoring as a window of three or four years.*

Carol commented, "The person I'm thinking about as a mentor is someone I met when I interviewed for a training program. She has helped me, I think, to synthesize both what I want to do with my life and the kind of person I want to be. It just so happened that she was there embodying both these things, the personal and the professional, at just the time when I desperately needed a model, or even the sense that what I was thinking about was somehow possible in the world."

A mentor may fade into the background when we're doing well, only to reappear at various times when we find ourselves once again at a moral, professional, or developmental crossroads. Sometimes it's the same mentor; sometimes it's a new one who better fits our needs at that particular juncture in our lives. By studying our own reflection in our mentor's reaction to us, and by being encouraged by her example, we're empowered to progress into the next stage of our development.

Sometimes the magic mirror reflects back to us our own image. Other times, the mirror goes clear to reveal new vistas and new possibilities beyond the structures of our present moment in time. Then again, sometimes the mirror turns out to be attached to a door, which swings open, allowing us to walk through into places we'd only dreamed of before.

Simone said, "My first mentor helped me to become more self-confident—to realize that I could and should nurture my dreams. My second mentor moved in the same academic world I aspired to join. She was really in a position to open doors for me and help me take practical steps toward fulfilling those dreams."

Through the Looking Glass

During Hitler's rise to power in Nazi Germany, Leah's family was precariously low on a quota list of Jews waiting for permission to leave the Third Reich. Despite this backdrop of political crisis, fourteen-year-old Leah felt profoundly alienated from her own family, never receiving the love and validation she longed for. When, out of the blue, a middle-aged Englishwoman named Mabel came forward offering to sponsor Leah's emigration to Britain, Leah felt that she was escaping from her mother just as much as she was escaping from Hitler.

Mabel was, in Leah's words, a quiet, unassuming Quaker woman of modest means who lived in a cold-water bedsitter—what we call a studio apartment—in London. By taking Leah on, supporting her throughout her years in boarding school, and spending every vacation with her, Mabel provided something Leah had never felt before. Leah referred to what Kate said when describing her experience with her mentor:

> *Those words resonated for me—"My precious girl!"*
> *Nobody ever said that to me or gave me that feeling.*
> *Mabel gave me the feeling that I must've had something*
> *good in me if somebody thought I was that worthwhile.*
> *It gave me a completely different view of myself. She*
> *taught me that I'm lovable—that somebody thinks I'm*
> *great. I remember opening a birthday present she gave*
> *me after she had begun to get to know me. It was a*
> *game and she said, "Oh, you're so good at games!"*
> *She really put herself out to please me, which was new*
> *to me. Nobody had ever put themselves out for me.*

Like Leah, Deirdre was made to feel special and worthy by her mentor at a point in her life when she felt especially hungry for validation. Solange, a well-established musician and performer from Europe, came into Deirdre's life when she was twenty. Now a professional singer herself, Deirdre said, "Solange was the first person to tell me I was special and make me believe it. I had always been complimented for my musical ability but not for the sound of my voice. She said my voice had a special quality, and this made all the difference in the world in terms of how I thought about my abilities from then on."

In her essay "Hannah Arendt: Thinking as We Are," Elizabeth Kamarck Minnich writes of the longing to be witnessed that was satisfied in her relationship with Hannah Arendt:

> *I just wanted to do my work and know that it had been understood, and judged, as it deserved. I wanted, and want my work and who I am to be seen. But . . . being seen is for me a rare and very special experience. I have had it from friends; from Hannah Arendt I received it for the first time from a teacher. . . . We must understand the stories of the women before us who were only rarely given the gift of being seen as they were." (180, 182)*

Dorothy, a retired employee benefits manager, described the life-saving dose of validation she received from her paternal grandmother:

> *I ended up with my grandmother because my parents divorced when I was three years old. My grandmother was born on an Indian reservation, a Cherokee reservation in Oklahoma, when it was Indian territory. Both of my parents were very young, and both of them*

were judged by the court to be unfit parents. So my
grandparents took me in, and they treated me like a
little princess. I wasn't this throw-away child. I was
this special gift that was brought to them in midlife.

Our mentors give us some combination of hope, encouragement, and validation that have either been missing from our lives or are in need of replenishment. In his book *The Uses of Enchantment: The Meaning and Importance of Fairy Tales*, Bruno Bettelheim writes, "The fairy tale begins with the [heroine] at the mercy of those who think little of [her] and [her] abilities, who mistreat [her] and even threaten [her] life, as the wicked queen does in "Snow White." . . . At the tale's end the [heroine] has mastered all trials and despite them remained true to [herself], or in successfully undergoing them has achieved [her] true selfhood" (127).

Caryn said, "It was a very long journey from the childhood in which I felt so miserable and hopelessly flawed to where I am now—a largely happy person, extremely excited about my life and all its rewards. I had to invent happiness for myself, with the help of my mentor, because I'd never seen it modeled before. And when you don't know what something looks like, it's extremely hard to find it."

When the Mirror Smiles Back at You

There is more than one magic mirror involved in the mentor-protégée relationship: in fact, there are two. In her protégée, the mentor sees a reenactment of some of her own youthful potential.

From the age of ninety until her death at ninety-five, Adele, a former fashion designer, was mentor to Ally, a writer and community organizer who met Adele while volunteering for "Meals on Wheels." Ally, who is now twenty-nine, talked about the mirroring that occurred in their relationship: "When Adele looked at me, she saw the girl she once was. And when I looked at her, I saw the woman I wanted to become."

When this sense of reciprocal identification occurs, it's all one and the same whether the mirror identifies the queen or Snow White as fairest in the land. Each gains in positive self-esteem with the other's triumph. Anne, an editor who has mentored more than one young writer, told me, "I can't imagine that anyone would ever question what she gets out of being a mentor. It's just so rewarding. I really feel that I get far more than I give."

Bruno Bettelheim reflects on this phenomenon as well: "The parent may suffer pangs of jealousy if [she], in [her] turn, has not succeeded in identifying with [her] child in a very positive way, because only then can [she] take vicarious pleasure in [her] child's accomplishments. It is essential that the parent identify strongly with [her] child of the same sex for the child's identification with [her] to prove successful" (207).

It's instructive to imagine a modern-day retelling of "Snow White" along these lines: On the day when the mirror makes its fateful pronouncement, the queen—instead of gasping in horror—smiles and says, "That's my girl!" She would then set about planning a spectacularly successful future for her protégée—a future that would, of course, link their fortunes and glory.

We are, in our turn, witness to what our mentor has achieved in fully becoming who she is. Our rapt attention, our admiration, our trust, and even our vulnerability are a flattering testament to what our mentor may only dimly perceive herself: that she has fully arrived in her own identity, and that this identity is an attractive one.

The mentor-protégée relationship comprises a win-win situation when it's functioning optimally. Kirin hadn't realized that her mentor was reaping just as many benefits from their relationship as she was:

At first I worried that I was taking too much in my relationship with my mentor. I couldn't imagine what I would possibly have to offer her in return for all her help. When I blurted this out to her one day, when we were taking one of our power walks together around the lake at lunchtime, she stopped dead in her tracks and told me not to ever worry about what I was giving her, because she felt that the relationship helped her every bit as much as it helps me. She said that for her it's a way to undo some of the hurts and frustrations she felt in her own career, when there was absolutely no one at all there to help her out or see that she got ahead.

Quoted in Susan Caminiti's article in *Working Woman*, Susan Grode, a mentor and partner at a Los Angeles law firm, says: "Look, I climbed a lot of mountains to get where I am today. Why should some young woman have to climb those same mountains if she can learn from me instead?" (69).

Validating Your Worth and Strengths

An effective mentor is able to reflect back at you an idealized potential version of yourself. She sees your strengths and is excited by them. Her keen ability to listen to you reflects her special gift of seeing you as you would like to see yourself. She is both magic mirror and witness to your identity. Your mentor's belief in you allows you to believe in yourself.

Edie, now in her mid-seventies, spoke about a mentor she encountered at the age of nineteen, when she got her first job in the social services department of a New York City hospital:

> *The young social worker I was assigned to was completely different from anyone I'd ever met. And it was that much more amazing that she took notice of me, because she seemed like such a queen to me—like an aristocrat, which she was, really. She thought I had some value, and her words really had a lot of weight for me. They changed my life twenty years down the line, when I was entering the job market for the first time after being a stay-at-home mom. She was the first person who said to me, "You can take care of yourself, Edie, and you can make a contribution."*

As the heroines of our own lives, we can encounter our validating magic mirror at any life stage. Hope, a retired early education specialist and preschool teacher, went to a teaching college when she was in her forties and returning to school for a Master's degree. A member of the faculty there took a special interest in her: "She saw something in me I certainly didn't see in myself. She changed the way I thought about myself: I finally believed I had something to say that was of value to other people."

Lori, now in her early thirties, came to see herself more clearly through the eyes of a teacher she had in elementary school: "Mrs. Stick made me know that what I wanted to be was a teacher. There was something about the nurturing I got from Mrs. Stick and the way that she made me feel like I was worthy of attention, like I was special—like I was fun and interesting."

Simone said that both her mentors, in different ways, helped her see how prejudiced she was against her working-class background:

> *My first mentor gave me confidence. She told me she thought I should be happy with what I had done and feel better about myself—that I shouldn't be so angry about where I came from. She decided it was time for me to really do something and stop talking about it. I kept saying that I wanted to go back to school, but I always had excuses—"I'm from this background. I can't do it. I'm not that smart." I had failed in school when I was at university in France. But she pushed me to do things. She didn't take "no" for an answer. She just didn't believe I wasn't able to do it.*

The belief that Simone's mentor had in her turned out to be well-founded: "I surprised myself, because after six months of my first semester at university, I earned a scholarship and I was on academic honors for all five semesters I was there." Today, Simone is in the middle of earning her Ph.D. in comparative literature.

Validation of our inmost desires seems to be at the heart of what the mentor gives us. Penny, a thirty-something broadcast journalist, talked about the mentor she found in her eighth-grade English teacher:

> *She really made me feel very special about my ability as a writer. She was able to help me see that I had these talents and to remember them later on. I studied psychology in college, then worked as a social worker for a number of years; but, all along, what I really wanted to do was write. And yet I was terrified to do it. Through the years, I've thought about her, about the way she treated me in class, and especially about what she wrote in my eighth-grade yearbook—which I was very sad to have her sign, because I knew I was going to have to go on to high school and never see her again. She wrote in my yearbook, "If I could write as well as you, I would be famous by now." Those words sort of echoed in my head. And now, all these years later, I've finally started writing.*

Penny recently published a well-reviewed exposé about the news industry, which she dedicated to her mentor.

Maggie, who was the first female book rep for a major American publisher, recalled the validation she got as a child from her sixth-grade teacher. Maggie grew up in a Northern California community where her Mexican family stood out among the mostly white, middle-class residents:

> *She made me feel important in the class. She would talk to me in Spanish. Nobody had ever done that before, outside my family. She would do it in front of the other students, so I felt like I was not only special,*

*but like I knew more than they did, because I had two
languages. Nobody had ever made me feel that way
before. Because of this, I really excelled in my class,
and I really cared about studying. It's interesting, in
a bicultural environment, what a difference something
like that can make.*

Tyler told me how her mentor first identified her as
someone special. "She took me under her wing. She
decided I was valuable, and it's made a huge difference in
my life."

A life-saving dose of validation from a mentor can
come at any time in a woman's life. For Edie, the validation
given to her by her mentor at age nineteen helped her well
into her mid-forties. But our mentors can bless and guide
us with their words from an amazingly young age, as Dorothy knows firsthand:

*My grandmother was a staunch Methodist, so we were
in church every time the door was open. She'd never gone
to school, but she had gotten her brothers to teach her
to read well enough so that she could read her* Bible.
*So she made sure I was at Sunday school, even though
I was just three years old. They'd give us a little snack
there, but you had to say a blessing before you got it.
And the only blessing I knew at that time was "Jesus
wept." The teacher said to me, "That's a very short
blessing. Don't you know something a bit longer than
that?" So I went home and told my grandmother that
I was embarrassed because all I knew was "Jesus wept."*

*When my grandmother heard this, she decided
to teach me the twenty-third Psalm. Three years old,*

> *I learned to recite the entire thing, because she felt*
> *I could do it. We went over it every night. She wanted*
> *me to be proud of myself in that classroom.*
>
> *And so the next Sunday, I not only recited the*
> *twenty-third Psalm in Sunday school, but the teacher*
> *was so impressed, she told the minister. Before they*
> *dismissed church, she said, "You know, little Dorothy*
> *has something to say," and I stood there before the*
> *whole congregation and recited the twenty-third Psalm.*
> *I felt really good about myself for being able to do*
> *that. It made me feel wonderful. The whole church*
> *was just so pleased that little Dorothy could do*
> *this, and I think that was the message my*
> *grandmother was giving me—that you never have to*
> *feel ashamed of your capabilities. My grandmother*
> *taught me that I had a lot to be proud of. She*
> *taught me that I was somebody important, that I was*
> *somebody smart.*

Dorothy lived with her grandmother until she was eight, at which time she was returned to the care of her mother and stepfather. She had five half sisters and brothers, none of whom were exposed to her grandmother's influence in quite the same way she was. Dorothy feels convinced that her own success in life was due to that early dose of validation her grandmother gave her—to the doors she opened inside her: "My grandmother certainly wasn't someone who was able to orchestrate things for me in my career—she never had a career herself, or any education. The most exalted thing she could think of for me was to get myself "a trade," as she said—something like being a seamstress—so that I wouldn't have to pick cotton or clean other people's houses for a living. But what she did was help me to be able to orchestrate things for myself."

Whether from inside or outside our families, mentors can both clear the path for us and keep us on the right path. Jordan is one of nine daughters in a family of thirteen children. A writer, counselor, and trainer for parents in recovery from addiction, Jordan told me how her mother—who was the first female postal carrier in the large metropolitan city where Jordan was born—always managed to find individual time with each of her children:

> *Don't ask me how she did it! Don't ask me—but she knew us. She knew who did what. She knew our strengths, she knew our weaknesses. She knew what we could do, what we couldn't do. She knew our teachers. She was at the school. I mean, it was like this woman would come out of the woodworks if we were in trouble. Mom would come up to the school. And that's the person you didn't want to come to the school, because she would go sit in the class. If you weren't behaving well, she'd hold your hand. "Okay. You need some reassurance. Let me hold your hand through high school." And it'd be like, "Oh, my God!"—but it would get us back on track.*

Jordan found a second mentor in a colleague after her mother's death. Jordan described how her new mentor helped her recognize her own strengths as a professional and come more fully into her sense of herself as a mature and accomplished adult:

> *Winifred looked at this training material I'd written, and she said to me, "Jordan, why don't you make*

> *this into a book? This is just what we need in the
> field." And I was like, "A book? Me?"*
>
> *She didn't come right out and say, "Jordan,
> you're good at writing and you should write." It was
> just that she was showing me a new way of thinking
> about what I do and about what I have inside. She
> changed the way I saw myself!*

Carol, now a therapist, had just embarked on her new
career path and was filled with uncertainty about it until she
met her mentor, who was her supervisor in a clinical psychology training program. Carol's background up to that
time had been in field biology. She attributes the ease with
which she took to her new career to the positive image
reflected back to her by her mentor, who convinced her
that she was on the right path:

> *Making the switch from studying animals to working
> with people led me to feel embarrassed—like an
> imposter. But Eleanor was so warmly open and
> intrigued by what I had done that rather than feel like
> I had done something odd, she made me feel in that
> moment, the first time I met her, like I had done
> something extraordinary. She thought it was so relevant
> and so valuable in some way. She also had a kind of
> delight in it—the kind of delight you take in another
> person's experience that opens your mind to something
> new. It solidified my concept of what I wanted to do
> with my life, and it helped center me in an area of
> work that fits with who I am—that feels comfortable
> and gives me a fulfillment I might not have found
> otherwise. She allowed me to blossom.*

Providing Encouragement and Feedback

In their capacity as magic mirrors, our mentors not only validate our most cherished dreams, but provide encouragement and feedback as well. Ursula is an artist and graphic designer whose youngest child is now in high school. Her mother, also an artist, has given her an encouraging nudge in the right direction at critical moments in her career: "There have been a couple of times when I've been at an impasse, in between projects. And my mom would say something like, "I really like your painting. Why don't you do more painting?""

Just as Dorothy's grandmother believed in a three-year-old's capacity to memorize and recite a lengthy poem, Rita was strengthened in her life and career by the trust and faith of her Welsh aunt. A sprightly and youthful woman in her early fifties, Rita is a primary school teacher and teacher trainer in the public schools. She spoke about her Auntie Iris, who'd been engaged to be married when she lost her leg in a riding accident, and then spent the rest of her life single.

Throughout her childhood, Rita's aunt, who owned and ran a little street-side candy shop in South Wales, gave Rita both encouragement and inspiration. Every summer from the time when Rita was three years old, she and her sister would travel down on the train from London to stay with their aunt and work in the candy shop as her "helpers":

> *It wasn't so much what my Auntie Iris told me, but how she was with me. It was as if, in her eyes, I could do anything. From a very young age, she let me open*

*up for her in the market. She would trust me with
anything. And she was so proud when I said I wanted
to go to college and be a teacher.*

When the magic mirror speaks to us, we listen carefully. The relationship between us and our mentors is so
finely tuned that a few choice words can end up reverberat-
ing for a lifetime.

Toby, a writer and healer, recalled the exiled Hungarian countess she met at a college in Alabama, when Toby
was young, lonely, and somewhat frightened by life. Now in
her late forties, Toby has a career that has spanned many
different disciplines and taken her on countless adventures
around the world. She feels that she wouldn't have been as
willing to take risks, and her vision wouldn't have been
nearly as expansive, if she hadn't fallen under the influence
of this mentor at a tender age. Even though Toby knew her
for an extremely brief period in her life, the countess's
words remain engrained in her memory. She repeated them
to me in a rich Hungarian accent: "You are not sure now
what to do with your life—it doesn't matter! *Es macht nichts!*
You are young; how could you know? Study, learn, learn at
every opportunity! Your life may depend upon a skill you
scarcely valued."

Charlotte, a consultant in her late twenties, told me
about a mentor she stumbled on when she took a summer
internship at a Washington, D.C., research institute: "She
would give me lots of verbal feedback about how I was at
meetings—lots of positive feedback. And she seemed to
have a lot of faith in me. I'd never really had any woman I
really respected in my life who provided that. It was very
powerful."

Betsy, an artist and graphic designer, described her relationship with the painter who had been the subject of Betsy's Master's thesis:

I was not in my early twenties, meeting a mentor and learning how to get along in the workplace. I had done all that long ago. I had a pretty good sense of myself. But these messages I got from Felicia were very important to me, because they made me really think about what I wanted to do and how I wanted to do it—and to think bigger than I had ever been able to think before.

The validation a mentor gives us can also be of a spiritual nature. Bridget, a professional dancer and dance teacher, talked about her relationship with her mother, who became Bridget's mentor in the final months of her life after a long illness through which her daughter nursed her. The mirror Bridget's mother held up to her showed a woman who had courage in the face of adversity. She learned not only about her mother's courage in dying, but also about her own courage in staying by her side. Bridget says that it's a lesson she will carry with her forever. The strength of her mother's spirit showed her the strength of her own.

Armed with a box of tissues, Bridget approached this painful subject with both courage and candor:

I only really got to know my mother before she died. I had been living out of the country for about eight or nine years, and I came back to take care of her with my brother. I spent most of my twenties in Europe, dancing—and she always encouraged me to go forth and do my thing. When she got sick, she still encouraged me. I just didn't realize how sick she was until it was too late and I had to come home. But still I had a year with her.

Being with her, and watching her world get smaller and smaller, it forced me to sit down and take a breath and be in the same room with her and talk to her like I never had before. She was, in this way, a spiritual mentor. I think the thing that affected me most was that even though her world diminished—from just the car and just the house and, ultimately, just her—her spiritual influence didn't shrink. It actually expanded. And through it all, she never stopped encouraging me.

Part II

Here's What You Get

4

*The Special Way Our
Mentors Listen*

By listening to me so closely and carefully, Sam was able to help me see myself and my potential with a clarity I'd never had before.

—Cathy

I'm pretty sure I would have given up and dropped out of grad school if it hadn't been for those late-night talks with Ruth. The funny thing is, she never said all that much during those sessions. She mainly listened.

—Sarabeth

Maybe I would have found the way without her, but I don't think so. And yet it's not that she pointed the way in any sense. It was more a sense of my seeing possibilities in the way she was living her life, and that uncovered something inside me, a sort of strength, a sort of determination I never knew I possessed.

—Simone

One of the most profound gifts that our mentors give us is their ability and willingness to really listen to what we have to say. Again and again in the interviews, women described the ways in which they'd felt listened to and understood by their mentors. These descriptions contained a mystical element, as if this listening involved much more than the physiological phenomenon of hearing and processing language.

This mystical aspect of the way in which an effective mentor listens has been captured in Diane Leslie's novel *Fleur de Leigh's Life of Crime.* The young protagonist says of her mentor, "To me, Thea is really beautiful. When I talk, her eyes never leave my face. She really listens" (280).

Mentoring is a buzz word in business circles these days. But none of the magazine or journal articles I was able to find on the subject zeroed in on this ability of our mentors to make us feel that they are really taking in both our words and the feelings behind them—even the feelings behind our silences.

While the professional literature emphasizes an active teaching approach, personal mentorship involves a deeper communication than a mere show of encouragement or transfer of information. Through their special way of listening to us, our mentors facilitate what can perhaps best be described as self-revelation. In feeling heard, we may find that we're able to hear ourselves for the first time. And because we respect and trust our mentors, we want to tell them the truth—a truth that perhaps we'd have trouble getting to on our own.

Cathy experienced this in her relationship to her co-worker, Sam:

> *Sam paid attention to these throwaway things I sometimes said about what I wanted or what I liked. And she built up a picture of me with this information that I think I never would have seen otherwise. Sam helped me realize that the way I saw myself was really different from the way other people saw me. I was carrying around all these old messages from the past and they were really clouding my vision. By listening to me so closely and carefully, Sam was able to help me see myself and my potential with a clarity I'd never had before.*

There is a genuineness to these exchanges that lends enormous weight to the mentor's words, even if she says very little. In these moments of truth, a smile or a nod can make all the difference in the choices we make for ourselves down the road.

Marcella also noted the clarity lent her by her mentor's ability not only to listen to her but also to focus on her strengths:

> *Because I didn't see my mentor very often, I was very attuned to all her reactions to what I said. When she reacted to something with a lot of enthusiasm, I enjoyed the feeling of these moments more than I care to admit. They stand out in my memory as moments of clarity and brightness, and I've used them as beacons many times since, when I've been unsure about which direction I wanted to go in my life or career.*

Listening Behind the Words

Alejandra, who moved to the U.S. from Argentina to get an undergraduate degree in psychology, described her relationship with her grandmother, whom Alejandra identified as her first mentor: "I remember when I was a teenager, my grandmother would listen to whatever I had to say with her eyes really open." Alejandra demonstrated by pushing her eyes wide open. "I noticed a difference between when she was listening to me and when she was listening to somebody else, because she was opening her eyes like she was really interested in what I had to say."

Many of the women I interviewed talked about how significant it had been for them to be listened to with respect, attention, and patience, without the other person making comments or offering solutions. For Sarabeth, a biochemist, being listened to by her mentor was invaluable:

> *I almost had the feeling that the atmospheric pressure in the room changed when Ruth and I had our talks there in the lab, during my first year of grad school. She had this special way of looking at me and screwing up her eyes, as if to say, "Okay—I know something's bothering you." Sometimes I wasn't even aware something was bothering me, but she would always winkle it out of me. We had these long periods of downtime, often in the middle of the night, while we were waiting for a sample to run, and if she looked at me in that way, I knew I'd better just take a deep breath and spit it out, whatever it was.*
>
> *I'm pretty sure I would have given up and dropped out of grad school if it hadn't been for those late-night talks with Ruth. The funny thing is, she never said all that much during those sessions. She mainly listened.*

Kirin told a similar story from the corporate world: "My mentor at work listened to me really intently, and this helped me articulate things I'd be unable to articulate in any other context. It was like she was somehow pulling the words out of me with some kind of energy or magnetism that came from her. I always felt the importance of finding the most accurate words to convey the truth of whatever it was I was feeling, or whatever I had noticed."

Maggie, who has herself been a mentor to many in her field and in her extended family, provided some explanation from the other side:

> *When you're a mentor, you listen to what a person wants, what they want to do. And then you help them see what qualities they have that'll help them get there—what the best path for them would be, based on what they've told you about who they are. I realize now that children don't want you to tell them the answers. They just want to be listened to. My nieces often drop by to talk to me, and they always say, "Oh, you've helped me so much!" But I haven't really said anything. I've only listened to them and told them what they've told me.*

Paraphrasing what the other person has said is another aspect of this intense type of listening—called "active listening" or "mirroring" by psychologists. In his book *Emotional Intelligence,* Daniel Goleman explains how an effective therapist attempts to reflect back to the client an understanding of his or her inner emotional state, in just the same way that an effective mother does with her very young child. This therapeutic replaying of what should have happened in the earliest stages of a person's development can give great healing. Goleman writes, "A patient may bask in the sense of being deeply acknowledged and understood" (102).

Not being mirrored as a child—or having one's feelings constantly dismissed or invalidated—can cause tremendous confusion later on. Susan, for example, was born in England during World War II to parents who believed in the propriety of concealing one's emotions and keeping "a stiff upper lip." Susan discussed how that philosophy has continued to affect her as an adult:

> *We were living out in the country on somebody else's farm, so we mostly missed the bombs and stuff. But once I was strafed when I was a tiny little thing, crawling around in the farmyard, and my mother actually took a hit on the shoulder when she ran out to get me. She still has the scar.*
>
> *A lot of different kinds of food were in short supply, and my father was away for most of the war. He was a bombardier, and I guess my mother never knew from one visit to the next if it would be his last. And yet when I said I was afraid, my mum always smiled and said I had nothing to be afraid of.*
>
> *It's taken me years and years of therapy and hypnosis and all kinds of things to even feel my feelings—because, early on, I learned to stuff them. By the time I was in my twenties, I had a hard time knowing what my feelings were about any given thing. And knowing what other people's feelings were was simply beyond me.*

Susan said that it was the experience of being listened to in therapy that made her realize how she'd never been listened to before.

Listening is part of the package of validation and acceptance given to us by our mentors. Kate, like Susan, never felt listened to as a child. She spoke about her mentor and twelve-step sponsor:

> *Celia had rather good parenting when she was growing up. She was looked at and mirrored. When she heard my story, it was really hard for her to get it, because her childhood was so different. Her father was a guidance counselor at a high school, and he actually listened to her every night. He'd ask her things like, "Oh, how was your day?" She would tell him all about it, and she grew up thinking everyone had that. She has very good self-esteem, and I'm sure a lot of that comes from being listened to so well. I never had one second of that.*

Being heard by our mentors can be a way of realizing how we really feel. This was true for Ally, who for five years volunteered for Meals on Wheels. Ninety-year-old Adele, who eventually became like a grandmother to Ally, was one of the people to whom she delivered food. Ally, in her early twenties then, was able to form a clearer picture of herself through Adele's eyes, and to articulate her inmost feelings by responding to Adele's questions:

> *Adele expressed her love by showering me with questions. She'd ask, "What new adventures have you and your friends fallen into? Did you work at the theatre last night? Have you been writing any more poetry? How are your mother and father and your precious puppy? Where*

are you travelling on your next vacation? How is your
job going?" And she always asked if it all "felt right."

Uncovering Rather Than Offering Solutions

It seems to be the special gift of mentors to listen in a way that lets us generate our own solutions to the problems we're facing. In Ann Gibbons' article in *Science* magazine, geneticist Susan Henry describes the mentoring relationship she's had with a number of grad students, who, because of their racial and ethnic backgrounds, "may not have had all the breaks or come from the best schools" (3). Henry says that she thinks of her work with these students as a matter of "cultivating potential." She doesn't coddle them, but instead guides them in learning how to solve their problems and achieve their goals.

Kirin, who is in her late twenties, spoke of the female executive who took her under her wing in her first corporate job: "There were many times when she didn't offer solutions to my problems and hardly even commented. But I knew I had her undivided attention in those moments, and just that in itself often helped me focus or frame issues in a new way."

Kirin and many of her peers have benefited from the female trailblazers who came, with a great deal more difficulty, before them. Gina L. Husby, one of those mavericks, is quoted in Cathy Cavender's article in *Working Woman*: "It's important that women help women; men have men to mentor them. It would have been wonderful to have had someone to talk to and get guidance from as I was moving up the ranks." Jackie McCurdy, then a vice president of another major American corporation, is quoted in the same article as saying, "I never thought about establishing an open-door policy, but when people ask, 'Can I talk to you?' I always say, 'Come on in'" (13).

Hope spoke of the mentor who helped her through her Master's program thirty years ago, when she was training to be an early childhood educator:

> *She has the gift of being one of the most profound*
> *listeners I have ever known. The school itself has*
> *Quaker roots, so that might have contributed something*
> *to this. She also strongly believes that each person should*
> *find their own path. She didn't require you to be her*
> *rubber stamp. What she did was facilitate people*
> *reaching their own goals, whatever those were.*

This special way of listening validates the reality of whatever we're feeling. If this happens in early childhood, it helps us to trust the reality of our feelings throughout our lives. Fran and Louis Cox explore this idea in their book, *A Conscious Life: Cultivating the Seven Qualities of Authentic Adulthood*: "Adults who have been allowed to mature listen to what their emotions are telling them, trust that information as real, probe and experiment with it, savor it, and share it with others. Emotions are just emotions, but how we react to them internally determines what, if anything, we're able to learn from them" (118).

Sometimes our mentors can also listen to the emotion behind our words, hearing more than we realize we're saying. Dorothy told me, "The thing about my grandmother that makes me kind of choke up when I think about her is that she could listen between the words. She listened very carefully to what I had to say, but she also knew what was underneath the limited words and feelings I could express as a small child."

Leah's limited capacity to speak English put her in a similar position in relationship to her British guardian, Mabel: "I have the feeling that she would never give advice to anybody, because I don't think she felt confident about it. You know, I think what she did mostly was support me. It was a very interesting relationship, because it was so quiet. It was just understanding without too many words."

The Nature of Nurture

We tend to think of nurture as something that passes from an adult to a child. But we continue to need nurturing as adults, both from ourselves and others. Our partners may nurture us, members of our family of origin may continue to nurture us from time to time. Our friends nurture us and we nurture them. But nurture, when it comes from our mentor, has a special sweetness to it.

Betsy spoke warmly of the nurturing she received from her mentor:

> *One of the most beautiful moments in my relationship with Felicia was very uncharacteristic. We were, I don't know, just about to walk out of the house or something, and Felicia was leaning on her cane as she always did. And just before she took my arm to go down the stairs, she stroked my hand, just briefly. And it was crossing a boundary, somehow. It was a very motherly, nurturing gesture, and very atypical of our relationship, which had*

*been very businesslike in a lot of ways. It makes me cry
now, just remembering it.*

Joyce, a writer, spoke of her experiences with the two
women who were mentors to her:

*Those little moments where they shared something
intimate from their lives or history have been very
important to me. I've cherished those special secrets
they've told me about themselves, when they've opened
up and been more personal with me, in the way that
I usually was with them. When those windows opened,
the relationship became more like a friendship. But
because it wasn't a friendship—it wasn't an equal power
relationship—it made it that much more special when
they opened up in that way. I don't even know how
to talk about any of this. I don't know what it means
or how it fits in.*

It's difficult to get a handle on the overlap between
mentoring and nurturing. Hong, a cosmetologist, explained
how her mentor was able to lend her maternal protection
and care when Hong was vulnerable:

*I came to this country without knowing anyone.
My entire family was left behind in Vietnam. I didn't
even speak the language. Kim was also from my country,
and she had a lot of family here. She said, "Come on,
you will be part of my family now." She encouraged me
to go to school and get my license. I was afraid to talk
to anyone, but to Kim I felt I could say whatever was
in my heart, even if it was bad feelings or anger.
Now we work together and we are friends. But at the*

*beginning, even though she is my age, Kim was like
a mother to me.*

The ways in which our mentors nurture and listen to
us have many of the characteristics of good mothering. The
crucial difference seems to be that we are being mothered
as adults, not as grown-up children. No one does anyone
else a favor by jettisoning her back to infancy or making
her overly dependent. But our need to be listened to,
accepted, understood, validated, and nurtured doesn't simply disappear when we reach the age of twenty-one.

As women, we're expected to provide all of the above
to those around us. Yet, as Caryn explains, this doesn't
mean that we don't need to be nurtured ourselves:

> *I grew up feeling like, whew, I haven't gotten enough of
> that for myself yet. But here I am every day giving
> something that I feel, inside of me, I'd still like to get.
> Becoming a mother didn't change the fact that I still
> needed a lot of mothering; but I didn't see any of that
> available to me. It was like I was just this big well
> that everyone was dipping into, but there've been so many
> days when I've just wanted to push them away. To say,
> "Hey! I need to get filled up, too. It's not just a one-
> way thing." Especially with young kids and a husband
> who's used to being the center of his mother's universe,
> that's a really hard role to play all the time. Like we're
> supposed to be these goddesses, who never have any
> needs themselves. It's just such a lonely place to be.*

For many of the women I interviewed, their female
mentors were water bearers to their wells—giving, listening,
replenishing, comforting, encouraging. Simone talked about

how her options in life were unleashed and expanded by her mentor's nurturing:

I suppose we find the people we need in life, and maybe knowing, really knowing, what we need is half the difficulty. My first mentor appeared in my life when I was really feeling stuck—when I felt myself caught in a sort of spiral and I could see the rest of my life stretching out before me as this terrible sort of gray expanse of disappointment and unhappiness. The way she drew me out of myself and made me remember my dreams completely untangled the spiral for me, so that I could see my life branching out with all sorts of new directions and possibilities.

Maybe I would have found the way without her, but I don't think so. And yet it's not that she pointed the way in any sense. It was more a sense of my seeing possibilities in the way she was living her life, and that uncovered something inside me—a sort of strength, a sort of determination I never knew I possessed.

Violetta feels strongly that there is some overlap between the nurture given by mothers and mentors, but that there are definite boundaries, too:

These have both been professional relationships, but they are certainly personal, too, and very important to me. I can't really separate my professional life from my personal life; what I do is what I am. These are both beautiful, wonderful women, but I would never ask them to, say, stroke my head in a way I might still enjoy being stroked by my mom. There's a maternal aspect to some of the ways they've nurtured and protected me,

even. But I never feel like a child around them.
In fact, as the years go by, I feel more and more like
a colleague. But there are still times when I feel like
a child around my mom.

Part of the nurture our mentors give us involves their acceptance of who we are, and the apparent enthusiasm they feel for this identity. Ally talked about how her mentor validated the excitement and potential the younger woman harbored inside her: "Adele saw in me endless achievements and possibilities, and she told me so."

Sometimes it can be hard to believe that our mentors are willing to give so much of themselves simply because they believe in us. Tyler commented:

It's a shocking thing, I think, when a total stranger
takes such an interest in you. We're such a closed
society, we're really suspicious of things like that.
We maybe think that someone's trying to get something
from us—you know, like they have an agenda. When
I got it through my skull that Janet just really wanted
to help me—that she liked *me—I felt like I'd won the*
lottery or something. Here was this totally great woman,
just everything I ever wanted to be, and she really liked
me and wanted to put herself out for me. It's just such
a great feeling to know she's there and always interested
in listening to me and hearing what I have to say.

5

*Mentors and
Tough Love*

The relationship usually changes in some way, either because of the stage I'm at in my work, or the stage she's at with her work or life. And then it's never just simple. There are other things, other interests, that get in the way. And it can wind up being really painful.

—Ursula

You learn a lot about your own power by feeling vulnerable to the power your mentor holds over you. And in a good relationship, you grow more, not less, powerful. Not in terms of dominating the mentor or anything, but more in the sense of learning how to hold your own.

—Paula

I really believe that we all have these helpers out there in the world. When we need them—and if we're ready to receive whatever message or help they have to give us—they appear; or else we find out that they've been there all along. Sometimes it takes an audacious act to make the connection. And sometimes the mentor is just standing there smiling, with open arms.

—Marcella

The kind of love our mentors give us is akin to what many experts feel to be an essential element of successful child-rearing: tough love. This involves providing a deep well of nurturing and validation tempered by certain standards and expectations.

Like a good parent, a mentor doesn't demand perfection of us, but she wants us to always do our best. She validates our potential, but she also has a vested interest in seeing that we live up to it.

The Double-Edged Sword of Expectations

The beauty of a well-functioning mentor-protégée relationship is that it's a win-win situation. Everything you achieve reflects well on your mentor. Your glory simply adds to hers. She gets a psychic commission every time you reach one of your goals, and she wants to see you stay sharp, self-confident, and unintimidated by the competition.

Cathy feels that there's an element of vanity in the pleasure a mentor takes in her protégée's accomplishments:

> *I've noticed in friends who are mothers that they have an unlimited attention span when it comes to discussing their kids. People love talking or hearing about themselves in just the same way. And it's the same, I guess, because parents tend to see their kids as extensions of themselves.*
>
> *Something similar happened between me and Sam—sort of a Pygmalion thing. In some ways, I think she came to see me as her creation. Fortunately, Sam*

*never lost sight of the fact that I have a life and an
existence that are completely independent from her. Still,
it definitely pleased her every time something good
happened in my life or career.*

In the sense that their love is by its nature conditional,
our mentors—at least those unrelated to us by blood—are
more like managers than mothers. Our mentors may nurture us and our potential with great patience, affection, and
even love. But if there is no payoff after what they consider
to be a sufficient passage of time, some mentors may make
the difficult decision to cut the ties that bind them to their
protégées.

Ursula, who has had a series of mentors in her work
in different artistic media, has found these relationships to
be double-edged:

*There's always a sense in which I fall in love with the
mentor. She becomes perfect in my eyes—it's just like it
was with my mother. This mentor's going to protect me,
despite whatever self-interests she may have. She'll
protect me in terms of wanting me to do good work.
She'll have my best interests in mind. She'll be on my
side, because it's in her interest to have me do good
work. But the relationship usually changes in some
way, either because of the stage I'm at in my work,
or the stage she's at with her work or life. And then
it's never just simple. There are other things, other
interests, that get in the way. And it can wind up
being really painful.*

In a healthy mother-daughter relationship, you don't
have to perform in order to keep your mother's love.

Bridget told me, "I guess a mother can't help but take you on—she has no choice but to take you on, nurture your spirit, take an active interest in you, and try to mold you." A talent agent, on the other hand, may nurse a client along for years; but it's in the nature of the business to cut one's losses after making what looks to be a bad investment.

Joyce recalls with sadness the turn of events that led her mentor—whose life Joyce was researching for a biography—to cut her off:

> *I heard from someone else, after things fell apart between me and my mentor, that she felt I wasn't "serious enough." I think she felt miffed because my personal life kept getting in the way of the work I'd set out to do in documenting* her *life and career. It's true that things were pretty chaotic and painful for me at the time—but getting dropped like that by her only added to the pain and confusion I was going through. When I left the man who was making me miserable, and had fallen in love with someone else, that was just another distraction, as far as she was concerned, from the real business at hand.*
>
> *I guess the truth of it is that I wasn't living up to her standards, even though I can find any number of reasons to explain why I probably couldn't have done things much differently than I did. I was doing the best I could, but my best at that time wasn't good enough. She was under no obligation to nurse me along. She knew better than anyone that her time was limited. She didn't want to waste it.*

Part of the unspoken bargain between us and our mentors is that we will try to live up to their belief in us. This knowledge of another person's hopes and expectations is part of what makes having a mentor so helpful. It can also be the occasion, as it was for Joyce, for a painful glimpse at our own limitations. We push ourselves because we don't want to disappointment our mentors. Rita commented:

> *Maybe we learn to love those people who are our mentors. I have another mentor, who is current in my life now. She leads a women's communication group I've belonged to for the last ten years. I really love her, you know, and it's that love connection that also allows me to admire her and want to please her. I want to know that she understands where I'm coming from. And I want her to know that I appreciate everything that she offers me.*

For Paula, learning to negotiate power relationships is part of the challenge of dealing with a mentor's expectations:

> *There is necessarily a power differential. I think that's one way we learn how to navigate our way through power—and power is a really important lesson in everyone's life. You learn a lot about your own power by feeling vulnerable to the power your mentor holds over you. And in a good relationship, you grow more, not less, powerful. Not in terms of dominating the mentor or anything, but more in the sense of learning how to hold your own.*

Demanding Our Best

Because our mentors may be able to see us and our potential with more objectivity than we can, the standards they hold us to may be higher than those we would set for ourselves. Ursula explained:

> *There was a period of about five years when I was doing ceramics. I was renting studio space from this incredibly talented woman who'd lived in Japan for years and studied with one of the masters there, and eventually she became my teacher. But before she took me on, she told me that I would have to destroy the first thousand pieces I made while working under her supervision. I'd heard of stuff like that before, but when it came down to the reality of actually doing it, it seemed really harsh to me. I mean, you put so much of yourself into every piece you work on. It took me almost a year of making and keeping things on my own before I started to see how low my own standards actually were—that I wasn't really growing. At that point, I decided to become her pupil, and we worked together for over two years.*

Sometimes our mentors may see a germ of potential in us that we've failed to see ourselves. Simone's first mentor nudged and guided her back into school. Her second mentor, one of her professors, saw in Simone a potential colleague:

> *She really pushed me, and she wasn't going to take "no" for an answer. She wasn't going to be satisfied with seeing me stop at my bachelor's degree. She told me, "I know you can do this, and you'll be cheating*

yourself if you settle for anything less." When I got my Master's degree, I thought that would be enough—no one in my family had ever even graduated from high school! But, no, she felt I should get a Ph.D., and not only that, but that I should only apply to the best schools.

Like a good coach or manager, our mentor may point out the ways in which we sabotage our own efforts. Tyler says that she felt completely overwhelmed by things that other people, from more functional backgrounds, seemed perfectly equipped to handle:

I wouldn't drive a car, for example, because I kept getting parking tickets all the time. And Janet pointed out to me—like, duh, you'd think it would be obvious to anyone else—that maybe I could just find ways to park legally. She actually gave me this little change purse full of quarters, and she told me, "You can look at the signs each time you park to see if it's okay to park there." It sounds so stupid when I talk about it now, but the idea had just never occurred to me.

Another thing had to do with the way I handled money. When I was writing checks, I never got that it was real—*that there had to be some money in the bank to back them up, or else they'd bounce. It wasn't that I didn't have any money. I was working and made a good salary. But sometimes I'd just forget to deposit my paycheck. So she helped me get a handle on some of these really basic, day-to-day things, so I could drive a car and write checks and not be in a constant state of freaking out about it all the time.*

In the essay collection *Between Women,* Elizabeth Kamarck Minnich writes about her gratitude for her mentor, Hannah Arendt: "It means a great deal to me that the greatest thinker I studied with, and undeniably one of the greatest of our age, is a woman. I now have no doubt but that part of the depth and range of my feeling for her springs from that fact. From the very beginning I felt a kind of closeness to her for which I had no grounds but that moved from being terrifying (because it was both so strong and so unexplained) to being healing as I have struggled to understand what she meant to me" (179).

Simone echoed these grateful sentiments:

> *I always remember who helped me, and that I could never do it alone. I'm lucky enough to be in touch with these two women regularly, and I tell them, "I couldn't do it without you." I believe it's really important to know that, that you can never do it all by yourself. It's too easy to forget, to think to yourself, "Oh, look how great I am, and I accomplished so much." But you didn't. It wasn't just you. Your mentor asked for your best, and that's why you were able to give it.*

"Still There For Me"

One of the striking things about the stories of the women I interviewed was the way in which their mentors not only showed up at the crossroads, but also continued to stay available for as long as they were needed. There was a huge range, though, in the time periods during which mentors stayed active in their protégée's life.

For many of the women, their mentor's appearance was fleeting, very much in the mode of a fairy godmother or guardian angel. Edie, now in her seventies, worked under the supervision of her mentor for less than one year when she was nineteen. Lori, Terry, and Iris were each mentored by a teacher during their passage through school. At the other end of the range were the women who enjoyed the continuity of a long relationship with their mentor, stretching out over the mentor's lifetime. Hong still works with her mentor and best friend, Kim. Marianna, Ursula, and Jordan were mentored by their mothers. Alejandra and Dorothy enjoyed this relationship with their grandmothers. Rita's aunt nurtured her hopes and self-confidence from the time Rita was three years old.

The duration of our relationship with our mentors, however, seems incidental to the transformative power of the connection. Marcella said:

> *I really believe that we all have these helpers out there in the world. When we need them—and if we're ready to receive whatever message or help they have to give us—they appear; or else we find out that they've been there all along. Sometimes it takes an audacious act to make the connection. And sometimes the mentor is just standing there smiling, with open arms.*
>
> *It's similar, I think, to the way people find a romantic partner. If you're not ready, you can go to all the singles parties in the world and not meet anyone. And if you're ready, you can meet the person of your dreams at a bus stop or on line at the grocery store. The point is that it has more to do with us and our*

*receptivity than anything else. There's certainly some kind
of projection involved that makes it happen.*

Not everyone takes such a mystical view of the relationship. Many women find their mentors within the more structured settings of work or the academy, where mentoring as a phenomenon has been to some extent analyzed. In an essay quoted in *Women and Work*, Deborah C. Fort and her co-authors conclude that "from graduate school on, women often lack effective mentors who can aid their academic careers, and few have worked with female mentors who might serve as role models for handling issues specific to women" (165).

A chorus of authors in the same book stress the importance of mentors to the institutional and career ambitions of women in academia. Robert Menges and William Exum say that "mentors function as 'gatekeepers' to professional advancement" (170). According to Thomas Matclynski and Kelvie Comer, women, and especially minority status women, are bound to lose out on the well-publicized advantages of the "old boys' network" within academia, because "members of 'colleague systems' typically choose persons most like themselves as their protégés," and "available mentor pools largely consist of white males" (170).

Violetta was unusually fortunate in that she found a mentor who was, like her, a Latina in the field of math education, which has traditionally been the province of white males. Violetta feels that that the whole nature of the mentor-protégée relationship is transitory:

*If it's not, there's something wrong. It all has to do
with when we're at these emotional or mental crossroads*

*in our lives and we need a guide or a compass or
a goad. But you don't spend your life standing at
crossroads. Most of the time, you're just trucking along
whatever path you've chosen during that period in your
life or career. Your relationship with someone who's been
a mentor to you may not end. My mentors are still very
important and dear to me, and I'm sure they will be
forever. But the relationship is going to change. It
evolves, just like a girl's relationship with her mother
evolves after she's become a woman and moved away
from home. You're still connected; but the nature of the
connection shifts and may continue to shift throughout the
different stages of your lives.*

Stephanie's mentor has been able to help her repeat-
edly in her career in filmmaking, especially because it's a
field in which connections mean everything:

*At first it was all one-way, of course, because I didn't
know anyone and she knew just everyone. All it took
was a couple of phone calls from her, and a project that
was only an idea a couple of hours ago suddenly had
money and energy and power behind it. Believe me,
I know how incredibly lucky I've been. This is such
a miserably hard field to break into, and all the help
she's given me has made me want to help other young
filmmakers in the same way. The great thing for me is
that occasionally now I'm able to make a phone call
that can hook her up with someone or something she
needs for one of her projects. I wouldn't say it's mutual,
because it's still—and I guess it will always be—very
lopsided. She has a much richer matrix of connections
to offer than I probably ever will.*

In Stephanie's case, the help her mentor gives her is immediately apparent and tangible. But many of the stories I heard reflected a subtler form of help and guidance. Edie told me that she really hadn't thought of the young social worker, Julia Goodyear Hearst, as having been her mentor until I asked her if there had been a mentor in her life:

Julia was always there as a wonderful memory, but I didn't realize until now how much of an influence she's been for me, and how, I guess, she really changed the course of my life. Some of the things she said to me just stayed with me more than anyone else's words have, almost as if I knew I'd need them later. And I did—over twenty years later. Is that being a mentor, having words that stick more than other people's words do? I don't know.

For Carol, there's an eternal quality to her relationship with the woman who was once her mentor, and who continues to hold a very special place in her life:

Eleanor retired soon after she gave me that much-needed dose of validation when I changed over from biology to psychology. I think she'd probably be shocked to hear that I think of her as my mentor, because it was all so momentary, really, even though it was so essential—so salvational—from my point of view.

She didn't retire because of her age, but because she wanted to be at home with her school-aged children, and I really admired that. In a way, I think of her as being there for them in the same way in which she was willing to be there for me. I so much admire the way she's been able to give equal importance to all these things in her life, all these roles, that are important to me, too—professional, mother, wife, friend. So much of the time, these roles seem in competition rather than complementary. But she has to keep herself vital in all of these roles. And because of the model and the hope this provided, I see her as still there for me just in the way she's living her life.

6

*How Mentors Shine Light
Along Our Pathways*

Her words and her kindness came back to me again and again during those last two grueling years. They were like a lifeline for me so many times when I felt that I was about to drown.

—Maria

She lives her life so fully in both the professional and personal realm, and it's this that has allowed me to blossom, I think. She gave a language to it. She made it solid, made me feel that maybe I could live my life that way, too.

—Carol

She cleared away some great, dark, ominous cloud inside me, a sense that even if things started to go well for a time, life was going to knock me down again—a sense that I was never going to be happy or succeed. And when that dark cloud was blown away, my interior landscape was more or less transformed.

—Stephanie

Mentors as Teachers

If teaching and mentoring were one and the same, we would all look back at our best teachers as mentors. And while great teachers deserve our gratitude for the service they perform, teachers and mentors are not the same thing—although they can be, in particular cases. Among the women I interviewed, Stephanie, Maria, Paula, Caryn, Iris, Penny, Simone, Ursula, Maggie, Terry, and Violetta all identified mentors who had also, at some point, been their teachers.

I asked Caryn, a high school history teacher who was mentored by one teacher in junior high school and another when she got her master's degree, to try to define this difference: What distinguishes a teacher who becomes a mentor to one of her students from the teacher who doesn't? Caryn didn't hesitate in giving her answer:

> *I've had great teachers who did the most terrific job imaginable covering the curriculum and making the material accessible and exciting. These are the teachers who really know how to engage their students, too, getting them more involved in the subject area than they ever thought likely or possible.*
>
> *The teachers who became my mentors went further, though. They crossed boundaries, so that I felt like I was learning about life and myself from them— not just math or history or drama, or whatever it was. It's a tricky thing, and I know this now because I'm a teacher, too. They crossed boundaries and touched me somewhere at my core. They made me feel like they really understood who I was and where I was coming*

> *from. They took the time to figure this out. And then*
> *they gave me the feeling that who I am is okay. A*
> *great teacher can cover her subject and engage you and*
> *excite you without ever crossing that boundary. She can*
> *change the way you look at things forever, but she won't*
> *necessarily change the way you look at yourself. That's*
> *the difference, I think.*

The women who identified their mothers or other relatives as their mentors described a learning process that combines both active and passive teaching. Their mentors lectured and advised them, but some of their greatest influence was simply the result of the example they were able to set in the way they lived their lives.

Marianna, an exchange student from Brazil, told me with pride about how her mother raised her and her sisters after their father dropped out of their lives. Not only does her mother work full time in the family business, but she also runs the household and manages to work out for a couple of hours every day by getting up at five in the morning. In photographs, she looks like her daughters' sister. In her early twenties, Marianna is on a career path in sports marketing, and is herself an avid runner and athlete. She said: "My mom is always telling me to be independent. Before I get married, I need to have my own money. I'm not going to be too dependent on my husband."

Mentors who do not have the pedagogical advantage of living with us for many years have less time to get their message across. Maybe this accounts for the heightened import their words have for us when they offer help and advice. Maria's brief encounter with a stranger provided her with a deep and meaningful experience of being mentored:

*I can't really say that I had a mentor in the way that
some other women have had mentors in their careers.
Being a lesbian Latina in medical school, I can't say
that there were an awful lot of role models available to
me. During my residency, though, on one of those
nightmarish shifts where I didn't get any sleep for
twenty-six hours, I was working in the ICU, and I
overheard a woman who was visiting her father there.
She was maybe fifteen or twenty years older than I was,
and she was speaking to him in Spanish, very tenderly.
While I was going over the charts, the duty nurse
mentioned to me that the woman was a physician.*

*I caught up with her at the elevators. I'm sure
the tears in her eyes were for her father. But, in my
exhaustion, I wanted to believe that they were also for
me—I was such a basket case at that point, and I'm
sure that everything I was feeling showed. She put one
hand on my arm and the other on my shoulder and
looked straight into my face with her dark eyes. They
were my eyes, and my mother's eyes, and my grandmother's
eyes. And she said to me in Spanish, "If you get through
your training, you will be able to face anything,*
querida"—*she called me by this endearment, even
though she'd never seen me before*—"and once in a
while, you will be able to save someone's life. Not
always, but sometimes." *She said these last words very
softly. The tears came to my eyes, too, then, because
I knew she was speaking to herself just as much as
she was speaking to me.*

*Her father died that night, and I never saw her
again. I never even found out her name. But her words*

*and her kindness came back to me again and again
during those last two grueling years. They were like a
lifeline for me so many times when I felt that I was
about to drown.*

Teaching by Example

In their capacity as role models, the best mentors follow
that cardinal rule of good writing, "Show, don't tell!" By
observing them, by interacting with them, we are given a
new set of choices about modes of expression and
behavior.

Alma, a teacher from Mexico who is studying to get
her credential in the U.S., was inspired by the teacher she
had from first through third grade:

*She was so kind to us! My brothers and sisters had all
told me how mean their teachers were, how this one was
a witch and that one was—well, they used all sorts of
bad words, so that I was really scared when it was my
turn to start school. I was so lucky that I got her as
my teacher, because she was so incredibly kind. She'd
teach us and she'd also touch us—it was like she
touched our souls. She really got to know us, and she'd
tell us all these wonderful stories from her own
life—happy stories about adults, about good things they
sometimes did in the world. Because of her, I so much
wanted to be a teacher.*

There are many lessons our mentors teach us by example. Alma learned about kindness. Jordan learned about the
essence of generosity. Even though Jordan's mother had

thirteen children, she would cook meals big enough to allow her children to invite kids from the neighborhood over for dinner. Jordan commented, "It's funny, because all of us cook the same way she did. We all cook *big* meals, and we're always ready to set another place at the table."

The unspoken rules a mentor conveys to us are sometimes just as important as the ones she articulates clearly. Ally explained:

> *Although it was never written or discussed, Adele and I abided by one very practical rule: we never said anything negative about ourselves or other people. Even though, in those five years, I knew she picked up on my frustrations and disillusionment about my job, my boyfriends, my life choices, she never gave me unsolicited advice. Yet by allowing me to be part of her daily rituals, to observe her with others, and by entrusting me to listen to and remember her stories, I can now fill a book with her positive life lessons. Although we saw the world from very different perspectives, we shared very strong values. She exemplified for me a woman who lived her life, in every way, her own way.*

Although Ally greatly appreciated who Adele was and continues to feel inspired by Adele's example of grace, courage, and good humor, the younger woman never lost sight of the fact that she and Adele were different people. As grown women, we have enough sense of our own identity not to want to model ourselves on our mentors in the way that a young girl, for example, might model her speech or dress after a particular singer or television star. In most cases, we're not trying to *be* our mentor, as much as we might admire her. Her gift to us is a vision of someone who is utterly true to her own identity and faithful to her own dreams.

Speaking of her mentor, Carol said:

She lives her life so fully in both the professional and personal realm, and it's this that has allowed me to blossom, I think. She gave a language to it. She made it solid, made me feel that maybe I could live my life that way, too. She lives in a way that reflects her values, and that's something I've always wanted for myself. But I'd never seen it personified before. I can't tell you the extent to which that has changed my entire outlook about what's possible for me—the sense that I can be a loving mother and, eventually, a grandmother, too; and that I can also be highly effective as a professional in my field. I felt such a depth of sadness before, because it seemed to me that one of these things would have to be sacrificed; that a woman couldn't do both, or couldn't do both well. And it's not that I put her on a pedestal, or that I think I should be able to be Superwoman or something. It's more a sense of seeing how she has modulated one thing or the other at various times; how she's managed things by being flexible in finding that balance between what's enough and what's too much.

Violetta's mentor helped her think about her profession as a math educator:

Sometimes I would use my relationship with her to better understand both myself and my profession in a true context. She gave me the opportunity to work in schools, to work with teachers, and to learn from how she does

*that. In my doctoral program, I was also learning theory
and big ideas from very important people who have done
important work, but not necessarily in connection with
actual schools. It was a really good balance for me to
continue to have this relationship with her.*

Not all mentors know that they are mentors. Mabel,
the Englishwoman who sponsored the emigration of fourteen-
year-old Leah, a German-Jewish refugee during World War
II, was simply doing what she believed to be right. As a
Quaker, and no doubt just because of who she was as an
individual, Mabel felt compelled to do what she could to
help others. From the way in which Leah describes her res-
cuer and guardian, it seems likely that Mabel saw Leah as an
enormous gift to her rather than any kind of burden. Mabel's
generosity has left a permanent imprint on Leah's life:

*Simply knowing what she did, that someone was capable
of doing what she did to help me, a complete stranger—
it has taught me how very much I would like to do
as much for someone else someday. I haven't yet; nothing
on that scale. But it would make me very happy to be
able to do so.*

Sometimes the example our mentor sets for us can
involve an attitude rather than an action. The antimentor
effect is very strong here as well: a negative attitude or one
that seems wrong to us can spur us to do something different and new.

For instance, we are enormously influenced by our
mother's example, even if the role model she provides is
one we want to be sure *not* to follow. Paula identifies her
mother as her antimentor—although she stresses that she

and her mom now enjoy a good relationship. Paula talked about her relationship with her mother, and how it has affected her hopes for her future:

> *I spent a good deal of my teenage years trying to differentiate myself from my mother, because there were so many things about her behavior I simply couldn't stand—not the least of which was her behavior toward me. I think it's been a defining mantra both in my career as a therapist, and as mother to my children, that I wouldn't be the emotional space-case she was then. I would be engaged and attentive; I'd work really hard at things. I'd be focused. Now I understand that, of course, I'm not going to make the same mistakes my mother made. I'll make my own mistakes! But she's really been a sort of touchstone for me in that way—and in a funny way I feel like I really have to thank her for it, for everything she did wrong. It's made me a much better and stronger person than I might have been otherwise—a better mother and better at my work.*

Dorothy expressed similar feelings about her mother:

> *She was a 1950s sort of woman who felt that a woman's measure of success, particularly a black woman, was not to have to work, to have a man who would take care of you. And if you had to go to work, well, somehow you hadn't quite made it. At the point when I announced I wanted to become a teacher, nobody in my family had gone to college, and only one person had even graduated from high school. The idea was totally foreign to my mother, and her attitude was, "What are you trying to prove?"*

A positive attitude, however, can be the proverbial wind beneath our wings. Dorothy went on to discuss the very different reaction her grandmother had to her ambitions:

> *My grandmother felt it was good to have your own money, to have your own profession—or trade, as she called it. She was much more open-minded than my mother was. Even though she herself had never seen the inside of a schoolhouse, she thought the idea of my going to college was simply wonderful. When I got my degree, and later when I got my teaching credential, I went down to Tulare where she lived, and took my papers for her to see. And she was walking on air, repeating over and over that her granddaughter was going to be a schoolteacher.*

Mentoring has become institutionalized in the teaching profession, which is plagued by a high drop-out rate among teachers in their first or second year. In many school districts, first-year teachers are routinely assigned to a mentor. This was the case for Lori, whose mentor guided her through her difficult first year of teaching English in an urban junior high school:

> *For about six weeks, Christine was in effect co-teaching the class with me, because I just was incapable of keeping the kids under control. Every day, it was very much a question of, what do I do tomorrow? I would go look at her lesson plans at 7:55, and then write the same agenda on my chalkboard.*
>
> *Christine has paved the way for this whole thing that I'm doing now, which focuses on reading. I'm*

involved in this research that's really cutting edge for secondary literacy. With two other people as well as Christine, we're putting the finishing touches on a manuscript about a whole new approach to teaching reading at the secondary level, and I'm going back to school to get my master's degree, which will center on the work we're doing.

Formal mentorships are also becoming more commonplace in the business world. In her article in *Working Woman,* Susan Caminiti cites a 1995 survey showing that 17 percent of participating companies had mentoring programs, and 35 percent were planning to implement them. A 1997 study found that 77 percent of U.S. companies that had formal development programs such as mentoring considered them to be an effective way to retain and improve employee performance. In the article, Caminiti writes about what she believes is a crucial element in effective mentoring: "The key to the success of any mentoring program lies in pairing the right people" (68).

While the pairing of a mentor and her protégée is sometimes done formally, often women find their mentors when they least expect it. Kirin found her mentor in a noontime yoga class sponsored by her company rather than through a formal matching program:

If Sondra were a man, she'd be called the "strong, silent type." I've seen her grit her teeth and smile or breathe her way through hundreds of situations that would have ground a lesser woman into the dirt. It's funny, because the first lessons in perseverance she gave me were in that yoga class. Some of the simplest things—just sitting on the floor on my knees—were so painful for me, I was ready to give up after the first hour. Here I was, half Indian, for goodness sakes, and I couldn't even manage the most elementary yoga postures.

I think she saw what agony I was in, and she took the risk of coming over to me when I was getting my stuff together to return to work. She told me, "It was really hard for me, too, the first few months. You might feel like giving up. But if you stay with it, you'll be amazed at what you're capable of doing." I had seen her before, and I knew she was way up there in the stratosphere, where the senior vice presidents live, and I thought, "Wow! I wonder if she's saying more to me than what it seems like she's saying." Later I found out that she had sort of scoped me out weeks before and had looked at my files and identified me as someone she wanted to cultivate for a management position. And it was in a moment when I was feeling vulnerable rather than competent or strong that she chose to show me that the door was open.

Bridget was able to observe her mother closely during the battle with cancer that eventually ended her life but not her influence. Bridget described her mother's last days:

She was still very interested in other people's lives. There were so many people who wanted to come to her and ask her for advice and just be in her space. I saw for the first time how she had a way of being that attracted people, even though, physically, she was very sick and very weak. That really taught me a lot, watching her. Somebody said, you can't love people for their strengths;

you can only love them for their weaknesses. My mother had years and years of raising me where she was healthy and vibrant, but right now I don't remember her that way. I only remember when she was sick, because I think that affected me the most profoundly When I picture her in my mind, I see a sick-looking woman—but, to me, she was the epitome of radiant beauty then. Even as her physical body became more and more incapacitated, her spirit's influence grew.

Teaching by Instruction

Although it's important to note the general distinction between teachers and mentors, our mentors do function as teachers for us. In the best circumstances, they teach us how to live our lives and stay true to our dreams. Jordan spoke with passion about all the ways in which her mother taught her to fulfill her potential, both toward herself and others:

She always told me I could do anything I wanted to. Anything. It didn't matter what it was—I could do it as long as I put my mind to it. She always told me that no matter what you want to do, you have to go after it. Don't ever not do something because you're scared. She'd always say, "Nothing beats a failure but a try." If you don't try, you'll never know.

I remember growing up with this saying in our house, "If you don't stand for anything, you'll fall for it. If you don't stand for something, you'll fall for anything. So you need to stand for something." She always stood for right and for helping people in the community. She had these really, really strict morals and values. My mom taught us that you have to be responsible for your family. You have to teach your children responsibilities, and you have to be responsible yourself.

My youngest daughter was born with hemoglobin C disease. They had to do a blood transfusion, which was so scary because of AIDS and all. I was so scared, but my mom told me, "When God gives you a child, whatever happens is His plan for that child. You just need to be able to walk through whatever it is." She understood the pain of losing a child. She'd actually given birth to eighteen children, but five of them died— a set of triplets, and then two other single births. She used to tell me, "Everything on earth grows with water—so if you don't cry, you don't grow."

Ally talked about the various ways in which her mentor taught her about life:

One day a neighbor walked by us and didn't say hello. I asked Adele if there was a problem. She replied, "Why should I guess what someone else is thinking? I'm not inside his mind and heart." Often she would announce in the middle of my visit, "I have surrounded myself every day with the people and things that bring me the most joy and love." Over coffee she said to me, "I love God and I listen to every person as if I have nothing else to think about or do at that moment, because all of God's children deserve to be heard and appreciated." When her body was failing and her days were tough, she continued to look out at the sunset and declare, "This is the best one yet!" I'd smile and say,

"Gram, you say that every evening!" With a twinkle in her eye she'd smile back and declare, "I do?" We'd both laugh and laugh and laugh.

On one of my last visits, Adele turned to me and said, "Ally, I have had so many wonderful adventures, and I have lived a full and complete life. Isn't that marvelous?" She smiled and gazed out her window, her ever-changing view for fifty-six years. She never stopped being fascinated by it. It always brought her joy.

In what they tell us, our mentors teach us to be more fully ourselves. Most likely, they are not teaching us to memorize important dates and places in American history or to conjugate French verbs. But the methods they use to get their messages across may sometimes bear a striking resemblance to traditional pedagogy. They may lecture us, offer us incentives and rewards—psychic gold stars for mastering the curriculum. When we're particularly thick-headed or simply stuck, they may hector and badger us until we see the light and come around.

Some mentors use the reward of greater intimacy as a spur to learning. Marcella said:

My mentor was a grande dame *in international circles, very respected and admired, and well-known by many people. She and her husband would host these wonderful dinner parties where you would run into absolutely legendary people in the world of literature or left-wing politics.*

I always wanted her and her friends to think well of me. There was a period of about two years when

> *those parties were the absolute highlight of my*
> *existence—this glimpse of a world I hoped, dreamed I*
> *might move in someday, a world of brilliant, witty,*
> *accomplished people who loved nothing more than a good*
> *laugh or a good fight for a worthy cause. Seeing her and*
> *her friends at such close quarters taught me a lot about*
> *the relationship between a writer's private life and her*
> *public persona.*

In their role as teachers, one of the most valuable things our mentors give us is advice. The word "advice" originates from two words in Latin describing the concept "to see what seems good." And that is what we rely on our mentors to do for us: to see into our future, based on what they know about us, and to make an educated guess about our best course of action.

Violetta, who was just finishing her master's degree in math education, found herself at a crossroads. She could leave school with her master's degree and teach math, which would get her immediately out into the community she wanted to serve; or she could go on and pursue a Ph.D. Violetta's mentor, who had herself stopped at her master's degree, had a strong opinion about what Violetta should do:

> *Her advice to me was that you can always teach. But*
> *going to graduate school, and putting in what you needed*
> *to put in to get a Ph.D., is something you may want to*
> *do now, before you are too immersed in the other things*
> *that will happen in your life—marriage and family and*
> *wanting some stability and needing the income right*
> *away. So I took her advice to heart, because I knew*
> *that it would be a long haul to get my Ph.D., and*

I knew from what she'd told me, and the decisions I'd seen her make, that it would be that much harder later on. It's a big quandary to decide whether you're going to invest that time and money and effort to do this. So I ended up entering a doctoral program.

For Stephanie, a filmmaker, her mentorship was a course of professional instruction and guidance:

I started out as production assistant for a big-budget industrial film Dana was making, and I was assistant director for her first and second features, which were both very bare bones, low-budget affairs, but very exciting artistically. It was like a continuation of film school, in a way, but it was so much more focused and concentrated and real *than film school had ever been. She was teaching me at every turn of the way—how to see, how to get people to work together, how to keep your overall vision of the film intact while keeping a dozen other plates in the air. I got up every morning so completely jazzed, knowing how lucky I was to have this opportunity. Our relationship has changed now, because I'm involved in my own projects. But in those early days I was a sponge to Dana's fountain of information and experience and ideas, just sucking up everything I could.*

Instruction by our mentors can be very practical and explicit, as it was for Stephanie. In other cases, such as Sarabeth's, it can be delivered in a more roundabout way:

Sometimes, with me and Ruth, it was difficult to see who was teaching whom. I was the grad student and she was the visiting scientist, but we were both the lone

*females in one entire wing of the lab, and that made us
a de facto team. We eventually worked on the same
project together, getting the lab's new mass spectrometer
up and running. I was more adept at tinkering with the
instrumentation than Ruth was, so I functioned as her
teacher for some of our protocols. But all the time,
during those long nights in the lab, she was teaching me
about much larger issues: what it means to be a female
scientist in what has been, until recently, completely a
man's world. What it means to try and have a normal
life as a young, single woman when all of your Saturday
nights—almost all of your nights—are spent in an
airless room, ministering to a big blinking machine
surrounded by toxic chemicals. Ruth was going through a
messy divorce then, and she was a little cynical about
being able to do it all. She'd always encourage me to
stay focused on what I was doing—not to try to finish
grad school and sew up the rest of my life at the same
time. She kept telling me to learn from* her *mistakes.*

Many of the women I interviewed had mentors who
helped and guided them in their careers. But what our mentors teach us may be largely unrelated to the work we do.
Cathy started out in a clerical position at the law firm where
she is now a paralegal. She was taken under the wing of a
secretary who'd worked at the firm since its inception, and
who taught Cathy about self-respect:

*Sam was from a working-class background, just like
mine, but she walked around like a member of the
Royal Family, and everyone treated her that way.
I was always trying to make myself as small as*

possible—which is difficult, considering that I'm
five-foot-eleven and pretty much stand out anywhere
because of my red hair. Sam was like, I don't know,
my ballet instructor or something. She was always telling
me to stand up tall and not to stoop and to stick my
chest out—I swear to God, she said that. This was a
long time ago, mind you. She taught me how to wear
make-up so no one can tell you're wearing it, but you
really look good. She taught me all these things I guess
I should have learned much earlier. The best word I can
think of is dignity. She taught me dignity.

I wasn't the only one Sam helped. On the day of
her retirement party, there were about twenty of us crying
our eyes out, including some of the partners. Sam lent a
certain tone to the place that we all tried to carry on
after she left.

Bridget's mom, who taught her daughter so much by
example in the way she died, also taught her daughter about
living life well and generously. Bridget described their trips
across the border from San Diego to Mexico, where her
mom went for cancer treatments:

We sometimes went shopping in Mexico before her
illness. She kept a change purse filled with quarters, and
children would just flock to her at the border. She had
so much fun just giving out quarters. I used to scold her
and say, "Now, you can't give money to everyone." And
she'd say, "Oh, yes I can!"

After she was sick, and she could only travel to
her treatments and back, the highlight of her trip was
always that stop at the border. She still had her change

purse, and she gave money to every child that came up to the car. It was the highlight of the trip for her, because she could still do some good in the world, even though she was so limited at that point by her illness. She would say to me, "As long as I have a dollar, I'm going to give it away."

Clearing the Rocks, Paving the Way

Besides teaching us, by example and by instruction, our mentors also open doors for us and sweep obstacles out of our path. Some of these doors and obstacles may be external ones: a mentor can make a phone call that may open a whole new career path for you. She can hook you up with an influential friend, promote your work, bring you to the attention of the powers that be in a way that creates entire new vistas of opportunity. She can soften the blow of any obstacles you might encounter.

After Violetta began her doctoral studies in the midwest, she realized that the program was not at all right for her. The contact in Chicago her mentor had provided her with before her departure proved to be a lifeline for Violetta in that miserable first year:

If it wasn't for her and my advisor at the time, I wouldn't have made it for even that one year. I knew very early on that it would be very difficult for me to continue on in that particular program, because I would probably have to sell my soul in order to graduate from there, and I wasn't willing to sacrifice my integrity or who I was as a person to do it. So when I was contemplating leaving the program, I called my old advisor one night, crying, because I just wasn't happy, and I didn't know what to do. I asked her what she thought about this other person we both knew, if she thought he would take me on as a student at the institution where I am now. Earlier he had said to me that if Chicago didn't work out, I should let him know. So I asked my advisor whether she thought he was serious, and I was sobbing because I was so incredibly unhappy. She said that she couldn't talk to me then, but to call her the next day. And so I did. And she told me, "Why don't you go ahead and contact him and see what he says. I think you should try to do that."

So eventually I ended up doing that, and he agreed to take me on as a student and I left the other program. Years later she revealed to me during the course of another conversation that when I called her that night and she said she couldn't talk, she hung up the phone and called the guy who is my advisor now, and said to him, "You need to tell me whether or not you're willing to take her on as a student, because if you're not, I'll tell her." She wanted to be the one to break the news to me if the news wasn't good.

Jordan, who is one of thirteen children, spoke of how her mother and father both created pathways and opportunities for their children and grandchildren:

My mom felt, if the kids were coming up, they needed to know about work ethics. She and my father opened some other family businesses, so that all the kids and grandkids would be able to work in them. We are still family-oriented, right to this day. We have an electrical business, a janitorial business, and a bookkeeping and accounting business. So the kids, if they want to, can go into those areas—they can learn them through the family. That was just the type of person my mom was. She had this vision of what she wanted and what she could do for all of us.

The rocks and debris our mentors clear from our path may also be inside us. She may be instrumental in helping us erase old tapes that tell us, "*You* can't do that! If you try, you're bound to fail." Cathy talked about how her mentor revolutionized Cathy's attitudes about herself, as well as her ideas about the way other people were sure to think about her: "I was used to walking into a room full of people I'd never met before and just sort of focusing on all the stuff I was probably going to do or say that would mark me as someone that no one would want to talk to after the first word or two of conversation." Although their relationship was an informal one, Sam functioned, in effect, as an unpaid therapist for Cathy, helping to build up her self-esteem.

"Transference" is another aspect of the patient-therapist relationship that has its parallel in our relation-ships with our mentors. In transference, the therapist serves as a stand-in for someone else in the patient's life, allowing him or her to explore unresolved psychological issues involving that person, who is most often someone from the patient's early childhood. For instance, in healing our relationships with our mothers through our mentors, we may find ourselves relating to other people in entirely new ways.

Paula described how her relationship with other women changed as an indirect result of the bond she'd formed with her mentor:

> *Most of my friendships followed the same pattern. I was inevitably drawn to charming but extremely narcissistic women. It was give and give and give and nurture and caretake—and it was all one-way. When I got to a point where I wanted the relationship to be more reciprocal, and if I dared say so—well, the whole thing would just explode at that point. I was the bad one, I was rejecting her, I was impossible, ya-dee-ya-dee-ya. It was me and my mom all over and over again.*
>
> *About two years after my relationship with my mentor began, I made this decision that I only wanted reciprocal friendships from now on. And so a lot of the relationships I'd sort of been suffering through for years just kind of fell away. And it was as if there was a vacuum created then, and all these truly wonderful people, both men and women, just appeared in my life. The amazing thing was that these new relationships— many of which I'm still enjoying—were all loving, giving, and reciprocal.*

Our mentors may also help us open doors inside us, doors we may have thought were locked, doors we may not have ever known about before. This was true for Stephanie:

> *Dana introduced me, directly or indirectly, to most of the people I know in the film biz. When I was raising money for my first project, she was burning up the phone lines and pounding the pavement right there beside me, helping the cause. There was something in all that good*

attention, all that validation, that, I don't know. It
made the sun come out inside me. A lot of seeds that
were maybe lying dormant inside me started to sprout.
She cleared away some great, dark, ominous cloud inside
me, a sense that even if things started to go well for a
time, life was going to knock me down again—a sense
that I was never going to be happy or succeed. And
when that dark cloud was blown away, my interior
landscape was more or less transformed.

Some doors are best opened. But others are best left
closed, at least temporarily. A mentor, in her greater wisdom, may choose to withhold information as a way to
shield her protégée from pain. Tyler told this story:

Janet's mentor role in my life was sealed when I got
pregnant. She was really supportive of my whole
pregnancy and really excited for me, and she was helping
me figure out ways to navigate through the pregnancy,
giving me referrals and things like that. I asked her if
she had a kid, and she said, "I had a son. I had a
son in '69." I didn't know what that meant—was he
born in '69? Anyway, I didn't press her about it. Over
the course of being friends with her during my pregnancy,
I kept asking her, "Well, did you breast feed?" or
"How long did you stay at home with him?" I was
getting bigger and bigger and bigger, and she kept giving
me really cryptic answers. I started feeling like maybe
I shouldn't be asking her all these questions. I thought
maybe I was just not being appropriate. I didn't want
to push her or anything.

Finally, I had the baby, and I brought him with
me to work to meet her, and she fell in love with the

baby. She thinks the baby's great. There I was, asking her questions again. I was talking about the rigors of breast feeding and how it's really hard, and did she do it? And then she said, "Well, I didn't want to tell you this when you were pregnant, but my son died when he was ten. He had a heart defect. I didn't want to tell you, because I didn't want you to worry about your own pregnancy, since he died of a birth defect, and there was nothing anyone could do about it."

You know, you worry so much about that stuff when you're pregnant. And she wanted to protect me. She didn't want to cloud my experience. And I just started hysterically crying. I was so sad for her, and I was so sensitive, and so protective of my son. But she said, "You can ask me about it any time. We can talk about it any time you want. You don't have to worry about that with me, because being his mom was the best thing I ever did." And what she did was sort of give me permission to enjoy my own son and not worry about her—to still enjoy our relationship. She didn't put any kind of weird, stilted halt on anything between us, and it was like a defining moment. I realized that she's really there for me. She's really on my side. She's not sucking up all of the world's energy. She's actually exhaling.

Part III

Mentors, Fairy Godmothers, and Wicked Witches

7

*Letting Our Mentors
Be Who They Are*

She'd chivvy me and advise me, but she'd also very easily take my arm when we were walking together, or accept my help getting in or out of the car, and it was wonderful to feel that she trusted me.

—*Marcella*

Everything she did and said during that first year seemed perfect to me, and certainly well-intentioned. It was only later that I began to hear how her wit could be very cruel sometimes…. She seemed to especially delight in shredding my self-confidence in front of other people.

—*Joyce*

I experienced her as the kind of person that I would most like to resemble. Her warmth, her generosity of spirit, the strength of her character and opinion, her devotion to what I thought of as being right and good—her appreciation for humanity and its extraordinary diversity.

—*Carole*

It's easy to idealize our relationships with our mentors. They give us so much. They have such a profound, positive effect on our lives.

But the truth is that the women who are our mentors have complicated lives of their own. Did you ever stop to wonder what the fairy godmother does with her time when she's not changing mice into horses for Cinderella?

We tend to think of our mentors in much the same way that children think of their mothers—as magical, all-powerful beings who are always there when we need them. We view our mentors as perfect because we need them to be ready at a moment's notice to perform a miracle. We rarely think about *their* needs or *their* vulnerability. Thinking about them as being any less than perfect is a way of diminishing their power to help us—and is therefore somewhat scary.

But our mentors are as weak as they are strong, and they probably each have a bit of the wicked queen in them, right there alongside the fairy godmother. And, no matter how old they are, they each have strains in them of all the fairy-tale princesses, too.

We tend to think much more about what our mentors give us than about what we give them—but this is also part of the picture that needs to be examined. Because our relationships with our mentors are so connected to our relationships with our mothers, the bond is equally complex and highly charged. The stakes are high in both relationships. Our emotional survival may sometimes feel at risk. For all the love we feel from our mentors, we may also feel a large dose of anxiety about the continuation of that love. Will she grow tired of us? Will we turn out to be a disappointment to her? Was her trust and faith in us misplaced?

Unlike our mother's love, the good offices of a mentor are optional rather than unconditional. It's not always clear what the course of the relationship will be as it evolves. The happiest course of this evolution seems to be a gradual shift from the role of protégée to that of friend. This shift can signal our progress from the crossroads onto the path of our choosing.

Violetta spoke about her relationship with her academic mentor as it evolved:

> *Our professional and personal lives have intermeshed in a way that could only happen over time. She knows things about my family and my background and my personal life, and I know her. She confides in me about certain things. Any hierarchical difference between us— any power imbalance—is just less apparent and less obvious as time goes on. I'm further on in my career, and she's further on, too.*
>
> *It's not to say that I won't feel equally vulnerable or needy in some area at another time in my life, or that there won't be other people who'll emerge to play the kind of role she did for me. But I think, for me, it has to do with a person who emerged at a critical juncture and helped me negotiate it in a way that has had a profound influence on the direction my life has taken. She afforded me opportunities and helped me grow and nurtured me in a way that was important to me at that juncture. And I still have a relationship with her now, even though all of that is in the past.*

It's a lovely thing to feel that even though you no longer need your mentor as you once did, she still esteems you enough to want to be your friend. As Violetta found, the power dynamic between you, which was by necessity unequal before, tends to become more balanced as time goes on.

But there is still something of a foggy borderland where mentorships and friendships intersect. In her article in *Working Woman,* Susan Caminiti writes, "Sometimes mentoring, like a good friendship, develops naturally between two professionals, each of whom recognizes a little bit of themselves in the other" (68).

This similarity between mentoring and friendship raises some interesting questions: Can someone be both a friend and a mentor? Do the two roles overlap at times? Once a mentor becomes a friend, is there no turning back?

Therapists have strict rules about this in their profession: no matter how great the affinity between therapist and client, the therapeutic relationship is sacrosanct. The boundaries of the relationship are completely clear and defined.

There are no such rules about the mentor-protégée relationship, and it's in these murky areas that we can sometimes get hurt or become disillusioned. It's also possible for a mentor-protégée relationship to segue quite naturally into a friendship, as it did for Violetta, with no negative consequences at all.

The Blurry Borderline between Friendships and Mentorships

How do you know if someone is a friend or a mentor? It seems that some women have the ability to act like a friend while serving as a mentor. In her essay "Hannah Arendt:

Thinking as We Are," feminist writer Elizabeth Kamarck Minnich writes: "[She] had an extraordinary gift for friendship, which I was forced not only to see but to accept. She saw people and liked them for their unusual qualities, not for their exemplification of characteristics she found comfortable or safe. Her friends and selected students were all Characters—well-defined people very different from each other" (181). For Minnich, friendship coexisted with her status as one of Hannah Arendt's student protégées, although she also notes in the essay, "I lived in terror that I would fail her" (181).

The imbalances in our relationships with our mentors can at times seem necessary to the flow of give and take between us. Kate spoke about the shifts that occur sometimes in her early morning phone conversations with her mentor and twelve-step sponsor:

> *I always ask her how she is, after we've spoken about whatever it is that I'm going through. But I recognize that I don't really want her to go into any detail. I don't want this to turn into a friendship. That's not what this is about for me. In fact, she's not someone that I would choose as a friend. I really want things to stay just as they are—to feel she's available to me in just the same way.*

Sarabeth's relationship with her mentor and colleague, Ruth, was a friendship from the start:

> *Because she's older than I am and was no longer a student, whereas I was still in grad school, Ruth was someone I looked up to in a very real way. Somehow, the fact that she was from Europe—from what I'd*

grown up thinking of as the Old Country—also lent
her a kind of status in my mind, as a kind of elder.
The fact that she'd already been married added to this,
too. But there's no doubt in my mind that, first and
foremost, we were friends. We were friends and
colleagues, too.

And because it felt so often like it was us
against the entire male establishment there at the lab,
we were also partners in crime, in a way. The friendship
we shared never got in the way of the learning part of
the relationship—although that part of the relationship,
where I felt like I really needed a mentor, was the finite
part. The friendship has lasted. Even though she's living
in Israel now, Ruth and I are close friends to this day.

Hong described a similar ongoing relationship with
Kim, the Vietnamese-American who was her lifeline when
she first arrived in this country. Kim helped Hong get her
cosmetology license, and now they work side-by-side every
day: "Kim was my mother at the beginning, and I was like a
baby. But the baby has grown up, and now Kim is my
friend."

Just as friendship can bloom within a mentorship, our
friends can also become mentors to us at times—just as we
may sometimes serve as mentors to our friends. Terry grappled with the distinction:

I feel as if I've been very successful in cultivating a lot of
strong friendships, with strong women in particular. These
are more reciprocal relationships than what I would call
a mentorship; although, at times, one person can be
giving the other one more. Maybe for a couple of years,

*one person's really doing something and the other person's
not in that space, and you're really learning from her
exposure. I think healthy friendships can evolve and
adjust. I had friends who had children before I did, and
they were much more in a mentoring role with me as my
children were born. But then, over time, I might be doing
something professionally that they can learn from. It kind
of ebbs and flows. I think the healthiest friendships ebb
and flow kind of nicely. It's not always even.*

The age difference between a mentor and her protégée can sometimes keep the relationship in an unequal balance, making a reciprocal friendship out of the question.
This was not the case, however, with Ally and her ninety-
year-old mentor, Adele. Ally said:

*Adele had a style and sophistication I had only seen in
fashion magazines. As frail as she was, she seemed to
float across the room, and she held herself tall and
proud. Our conversation and our unique friendship would
continue on almost a daily basis for the next five years,
as would our rituals. We enjoyed our paella dinner
birthday celebrations, writing funny letters to her stepson
and grandchildren who lived abroad, sneaking food to the
cat who lived in the laundry room, taking walks together
in the neighborhood, watching fireworks every July fourth
on the roof of her building, and sitting in comfortable
shared silence on her black couch, sipping glasses of
ginger ale and watching the sunset behind Adele's
beautiful hand-painted silk curtains.*

*I became Adele's adopted granddaughter and her
girlfriend, but since her recent death, I now refer to her*

as my "Life Mentor." We delighted in each other's company, we learned from each other, and if giggling were made illegal, we would have been issued many, many tickets from the giggle police.

The difference in age and perhaps professional status was more of an issue for Marcella:

I was too much in awe at the beginning to even entertain the idea that my mentor might think of me as a friend. And I wasn't a friend in the way that some of her contemporaries or other old pals were—they'd gone through so much together, and I was such a recent acquisition. Because of the nearly forty-year age difference between us, I would always be, at best, her young *friend.*

As things wore on and we spent more time together, she opened up more and more about her own life and her own take on very personal things—her drinking, for one, and the whole history of how she stopped. She also told these hilariously funny stories about herself, about how hopeless she was as a mother before her children were grown. But there were certain places she never went with me. Part of this had to do simply with who she was—she wasn't a person who enjoyed or even thought it proper to talk about our own private miseries. She was very much of the stiff-upper-lip school of life.

It was when we were being outrageous in public together—talking our way into seats at the mayor's table, that sort of thing—that we came closest, I think, to feeling like a couple of friends. There was a lot of mother-daughter, even grandmother-granddaughter stuff

*between us, too. She'd chivvy me and advise me, but
she'd also very easily take my arm when we were
walking together, or accept my help getting in or out
of the car, and it was wonderful to feel that she
trusted me.*

*I think I felt her to be so much a part of
my extended family that it hurt on some level that I
wasn't one of the people asked to be around her
bedside when she was dying—even though it was all
very old friends and real family, and I probably would
have been hopelessly weepy, which was exactly what she
didn't want. I arranged an enormous bouquet of flowers
for her, and wrote her what I'm sure she thought of
as an insufferably sentimental letter, telling her how
much our friendship has meant to me. I had to tell
her, even though I felt pretty strongly that she wouldn't
at all approve.*

It seems that some mentors can segue into a friendship, while preserving their mentor role for times of need.
Caryn told me:

*I think there's a very natural shift as you move from
one stage of your career or whatever into the next one.
Both my mentors were there for me at times when I was
either confused about what I wanted to do, or else felt
discouraged about going on. I've lost touch with the
earlier one, and I kind of regret that now. But my
mentor from my master's program is definitely one of my
friends now. For a while, we were colleagues at the same
school, and that pretty much cemented things between
us. But she's still one of the first people I call when*

I run into a teaching- or bureaucracy-related problem.
She knows the ropes, she's been through it all, and
I know she always has my best interests at heart.

Snuffing Out the Candles
and Turning Up the Lights

Besides their parallels with the mother-daughter relationship, mentor-protégée dyads share certain similarities with
the realm of romantic love. When we first encounter our
mentor and are taken under her wing, we may feel much of
the same sense of wonder, admiration, grace, and awe that a
person feels upon falling in love.

Everything is lit by a special light when we fall in love.
Our pupils dilate so that we can take in as much of the
sight of our beloved as we possibly can. Time itself flies off
its hinges. Sleep becomes something we do for the pleasure
of waking up and seeing our beloved's face again.

Ursula's story illustrates this parallel. She met a fellow
artist who became a mentor to her during a stint as one of
seven designers making greeting card templates for a paper
company. The woman who became her mentor was also
her supervisor:

We developed a relationship where I stopped off at her
house, we socialized. We had times where we were so
excited over the work that we forgot we were working
together. We were just saying, "Oh, this is so cute!
People are gonna love this!"

So, first, you're in love. You feel like this person
really understands you, really helps you, and is on your

side—you feel like a couple. You're going up together. You help her, and she helps you. That's the first bloom. Then maybe there are conflicts. In our case, the company was sold, the whole corporate culture changed, and she was too naive to realize what was happening—that the designers had just become slave labor.

I was sympathetic toward her, but also I felt that she was no longer on my side. She was beleaguered by changes in her life, and that made her unable to be a friend. She wanted to be, but she couldn't. I've always felt a lot of sympathy and given a lot of leeway to the mentors I've had who've had to drop me or who've had to go their own way. I don't feel angry with them, though there is a part of me that must be. I accept their reality, that they have to choose between me and their own interests—and they have to choose their own interests, ultimately. That's just the way it works.

Having a mentor is not exactly the same as falling in love, to be sure. But we do tend to see the woman who takes us under her wing in a very special and flattering light, a psychic candlelight or moonlight in which none of her faults or frailties show at all (or in which they appear mysteriously beautiful). Our pupils are wide open in this low light, and our ears are attuned to whatever she says to us, prepared to take in and remember her every word and gesture. And time flies off its hinges in that our mentor's words will be clearly audible to us and her expression clearly remembered even after years and years. Like a poem memorized in childhood, her words will stay with us forever—unlike the millions of other words spent and spoken, which simply evaporate and disappear.

We all know what happens, however, in the latter stages of a romantic relationship. It's during this time that the love madness eases up somewhat and we begin to see the object of our affection in a brighter, sometimes less forgiving light.

Charlotte spoke about how an academic mentor eventually emerged into the light as a whole human being, with all her human frailties visible:

> *Connecting with other students who had a similar experience helped me get some perspective on her as a person. When you idealize people, it hurts so much when you realize they're just people. You may have heard things about their faults, but maybe you didn't listen or didn't want to listen.*
>
> *Once I started to connect with other people who'd had similar experiences, I remembered things people had said about her in other contexts, and they started to ring true for me. I thought, oh, that's what they were talking about! It started to open the gate to really seeing her as a whole person. You know? I really think that's where it's at. You just can't idealize people and expect them to be this perfect being, you know, one hundred percent in touch with everything and able to address all your needs. They're going to have to emerge as people eventually; and then you're going to be disappointed. There I was, young and naive and kind of looking up to people. Now I think I'm a little more cautious. I think I've had it happen enough now so that I won't fall into that trap as easily again.*

Joyce's experience of seeing her mentor in a more realistic light was quite painful:

During that entire first year of my visits, it felt like
I was stepping into an exquisite painting. Everything
glowed—her pink cheeks, the flowers in vases, the
conversation. It's funny, because in my memory it's
always either sunset or dawn there, and the light is
pinkish and gold. I know that's crazy, because most
of my visits were in summer, and it gets broiling hot
there in the summertime. She never seemed hot, though.
I see her with a glass of chilled Chardonnay in her
hand, sitting in her big wing chair looking out toward
the sunset.

Everything she did and said during that first year
seemed perfect to me, and certainly well-intentioned. It
was only later that I began to hear how her wit could
be very cruel sometimes. I saw how isolated she was out
there, in a way, even though people were always flocking
in to visit her; how stuck she must have felt in her old
lady's body with her frail legs and shaking hands and
failing voice. There were times when I was nothing more
than a mouse that had made the mistake of venturing
into a house possessed of a large, skillful cat. I still felt,
at that point, so dependent on her kindness. But when
she felt especially ill, or maybe she'd had too much to
drink or had mixed her drinks badly with her
medications, I felt so vulnerable to her sudden shifts of
mood and the desperate sense of anger behind them. She
seemed to especially delight in shredding my self-confidence
in front of other people.

After a very short time of this, I stopped visiting;
and about a year later, she died. It was all very sad for
me, and it made me rather gun-shy about making myself

so vulnerable again. I felt sure that there was some way in which I had brought it all on myself by not seeing her more clearly at the beginning, and never questioning why she was so willing to have me around. It was a complex situation, but I had refused to see it that way.

Disillusionment isn't always as dramatic or painful as it was in Joyce's case. For Stephanie, there was simply a gradual dawning of reality:

It's dog-eat-dog in the film biz, and there's always going to be a certain amount of backstabbing. When I first started working with Dana, I thought she could do no wrong. Eventually I found out that she sometimes could. But expecting anything more—or less—would really be unfair. I don't know anyone who's perfect all the time, do you?

Tyler put it especially well:

When you're in a relationship with anyone, if it's more than a one-night stand, you're going to find out about things you don't like all that much in the other person. It's true with someone you're involved with romantically, it's true with friends, it's true with family members, and it's true with mentors, too. With family members, you don't have much choice, because you're kind of stuck with each other. But in every other kind of relationship, you get to weigh the things you like against the things you don't like, and figure out if it's a balance you can live with.

In my own particular case, I've got to admit that my mentor still seems pretty much perfect to me—but the relationship hasn't been going on all that long, and we don't see each other all that often. But I like feeling so starry-eyed. It makes the world seem like a better place to me.

Charlotte had no expectations about her second mentor, which made it easier for her to accept her mentor for who she was:

I think that helped, because I really got to know her as a person. After a while, she let me into this other side of her, too, her witchy side, which I thought was really interesting. I had never really known a witch before. She would do Tarot readings for me, and kind of give me guidance through Tarot—which was so far afield from the very straight-laced nonprofit fundraising world we were working in. She understood my desire to pursue being more oriented toward activism in my life; she helped me think through that process. Eventually, we just became like family.

Violetta spoke of a temporary falling out with one of her academic mentors:

I had just broken up with the man I had thought I was going to marry. I was devastated, because all signs indicated that we were going to get married and have children. And when I talked to her about it, one of her comments to me was, "Don't define yourself by being a wife and having a family." And I thought, well, that's easy for her to say because she's married and has children. That was very difficult for me to handle,

because having a family and sharing my life with someone was a really important aspect of what I wanted to
do. I never thought I defined myself by that, but it was
an important thing. It was hard for me to have her say
that, especially because she had been in a marriage for a
long time and had two adorable children.

It created this awkwardness we had never
experienced before. We ended up talking about what
happened. It was probably what you'd think of as a
first major fight. It hurt me, and it hurt her, too. And
in the end we realized that this was probably going to
happen again. It happens with your family, it happens
with your friends. You're going to have these misunder-
standings. It's how you move on from there, and what
you learn about each other and yourself, that determines
the value of the experience and, ultimately, the relationship.

Like Violetta, Dorothy expressed an easiness about
looking at her mentor realistically without feeling that the
relationship was compromised:

My grandmother was very definitely on a pedestal, when
I was so young and so vulnerable, from the time I was
three till when I was eight. But as I got older, I could
see that she had feet of clay, too. She was very
superstitious. You drop a fork, a woman's coming to
visit. You drop a knife, a man's coming to visit. When
I told her who I was marrying, she said, "Oh, shit."
Those were her exact words. And I said, "Grandma,
why would you say that?" And she answered, "Well,
his ears are too small. He's stingy." That was my first
husband, and it turned out that she was pretty much

right. And then I had to come back and eat a little humble pie.

But the thing about my grandmother is, she didn't have a sense of humor. She picked cotton all day, and then she came home and took care of a three-year-old child and cleaned the house and raised chickens and pigs and tended the garden. She made her own soap! Every minute was work. You sat down and made quilts to relax. But you're always engaged in using your time productively, usefully, and even now I find it hard to just sit and wool-gather or just not be doing something. If I'm watching TV, I'm knitting. I feel like I've got to come up with an end product, you know? She gave me invaluable lessons in my life, and there was also a certain rockiness to the relationship—I realized that there were some things I had to get from sources other than her. But I think that's fine.

Unfortunately, she died before I married my second husband. She would have liked him. He's got big ears, for one thing!

There are some mentor-protégée relationships that don't involve the danger of a big romantic falling-out, just because they last for a very short time. Tyler speculated about this:

I guess, in some cases, maybe people don't ever get to know their mentors that well. They don't ever see the three dimensions or all the complexities, but the person has still had a very positive influence on them, and that influence isn't diminished by the fact that you never got to know the whole person that intimately. Maybe these kind of mentorships are like one-night stands. And then there are these other kinds of relationships where you really connect as friends. You really know each other well, and the connection develops into a multifaceted relationship, a lifelong relationship that will continue to influence you in a lot of different ways.

Mentors, Fairydust, and Never-Neverland

For all their frail humanity and their feet of clay, our mentors still possess the fairydust that makes us fly. For many of the women I interviewed, it seemed a source of satisfaction to them that they could see their mentors clearly as human beings, warts and all, while still appreciating how much these women had helped them in their lives.

Simone readily admits that she has been transformed—and her life has certainly been turned upside down—as a direct result of the fairydust sprinkled on her by her mentor some five years ago. She's no longer stuck in the unhappy marriage that had made her feel middle aged much before her time. She's amicably coparenting her daughter now with her ex-husband, she feels terrific, and she's thriving in her Ph.D. program. Simone still stays in close touch with the person who was the catalyst for all of these changes:

> *She was really happy when I got into the program, because it was actually a reflection on her. It was like a piece of work she'd completed. She showed me that it was possible to come from almost nothing and accomplish*

a lot if you had the confidence and the people behind you. I've always been very lucky in that way, meeting the right women.

What started out as a Master's thesis for Betsy turned into a relationship that has had a profound impact on her life and career:

I got to know her over a period of about a year, working on this project. She was in some sense an authority figure for me, and she was crucial to my finishing my program. And yet it was not a traditional work situation of any kind. I interviewed her a number of times over the course of several months, always at her home, and so I was gradually introduced to her husband, her daughter, and a couple of other people. But, really, it was a fairly formal relationship during that time.

Once I finished my program the following summer and finished the thesis and so on, she made it clear to me that she liked what I'd written and enjoyed some of the things I said in there. She had copies made and sent them around to her friends, including one of her old editors—so that was very flattering.

At that point, she reached out to me and took an interest in what I was going to do next. She began inviting me to these famous parties at her house that were full of luminaries. There were always amazing people there from the art world. And she also asked me to accompany her a couple of times when she was going to events—luncheons and gallery openings and that sort of thing—and she'd introduce me around. I didn't know quite what to make of all this, but I certainly welcomed that lengthening of our relationship beyond the scope of my original project.

Because I studied her life so closely, almost in a biographical sense, in the course of writing my thesis, I really got a chance to make my own interpretations about how she has gotten where she is today. I mean, here she was, this locally and nationally beloved figure who had many, many friends in the art world, especially in New York, and also had strong ties to the midwest, and practically knew everybody. She seemed full of confidence and had this incredible wit and so on, but I knew that she hadn't always been confident and that she spent a long time very interested and active in the art world but was not really sure about what her own contribution would be.

I took a lot of interest in how she really pulled herself up by the bootstraps to accomplish a lot of things that she never thought possible at first. She was a frequent speaker in all kinds of venues, and I always thought, oh, she just gets up there and rattles it off. It looks so easy. But it wasn't easy for her. It got easier later in life, but she prepared very, very carefully and was very exacting in trying to get it just right. These were all messages that were very meaningful to me.

After we've moved beyond infatuation to insight into our mentors, we can sometimes find instructive life lessons in their mistakes as well as their triumphs, and in their frailties as well as in their strengths. Ursula spoke about the ways in which her mother's lack of follow-through as an artist has inspired Ursula to pay close attention to her own work habits:

> *My mom has ideas that inspire her, and she gets very excited and works very hard at the beginning—and then the work becomes more and more funky at the end. She sees the idea in her mind and she really wants to go for it. But the way she has sabotaged herself is to use low-grade materials sometimes, and to not have things framed properly, and to do things so that, by the end, they are less than professional-looking. That became something I had to overcome in my own work. I found that I had to work really, really hard, and sometimes do something over and over again, before I got it right.*

Our mentor's influence exists in a kind of Never-Neverland where very little changes. We can return there whenever we want to by invoking her memory. Speaking of her mentor, Carol said:

> *I experienced her as the kind of person that I would most like to resemble. Her warmth, her generosity of spirit, the strength of her character and opinion, her devotion to what I thought of as being right and good— her appreciation for humanity and its extraordinary diversity. These are things that have stayed with me through all my years in this field, and I feel certain they'll stay with me throughout the rest of my life, even if at some point I stop working.*
>
> *There's a way in which I can think about her and call to mind all the values she stands for. It's an immediate association, and it can sometimes completely*

shift the course of something for me if I'm faced with a conflict or even a sense of boredom in a given moment. Invoking those values infuses everything with a deeper meaning, and has a way of increasing my engagement with whatever is at hand.

8

*The Magic Merge:
Internalizing Our
Mentor's Voice*

This doesn't mean that I necessarily follow her vision rather than my own. I mean, I never do, not at this point. But I carry her around inside me like an extra pair of eyes.

—Stephanie

Because I chose to retire early and wasn't out there tilting at windmills anymore, I had assumed that she disapproved of the path I had taken. And I realized after a conversation with her that this was pure projection. It was obvious from the warmth in her voice; I felt certain that we were old friends again, and that felt so wonderful because we always had such a close, caring feeling about each other.

—Hope

I still draw on her strength and her wit and the tremendous sense in which she was always ready to stand up for something or someone she believed in.

—Marcella

In their capacity as role models and teachers, our mentors bequeath to us a more expansive view of ourselves and a broader vision of what we might accomplish in the world. They bolster our self-confidence and school us in self-acceptance. By taking on some of the psychological significance of a mother, they can help us complete any leftover developmental business that may have been compromising our adult relationships with female relatives and friends.

We bloom in the light of our mentors' influence, because they demand our best. They teach us to solve our own problems. Even if we've been hurt by others in the past, their belief in us and their constancy open us to the idea of trusting and being nurtured by another human being.

In her essay "Hannah Arendt: Thinking as We Are," Elizabeth Kamarck Minnich writes, "I cannot begin to say all I learned from Hannah Arendt because I think with her all the time and will always do so. But Hannah Arendt, simply by being there and accepting me, freed me...I am more grateful than I can possibly say that she was in the world and that I have her with me, always, whenever I find the courage to think" (184–185).

Ally's story stands as an apt metaphor for the ways in which we learn to see through our mentor's eyes:

> *When Adele died, her grandson asked me if I wanted any of her things. I took two momentos: her guest book, where many friends left loving messages after paying a visit, and the hand-painted silk curtains through which she looked out at the city. When I miss Adele, I leaf through the guest book and recall all of our special times*

together. And the curtains? Well, in sixty-one years
I'll be sitting somewhere on a black couch, facing those
curtains and enjoying it all over again—from the
other side.

Once she's left her mark on us, a mentor's influence
can be as powerful after her death as it was during her lifetime. Marcella said:

There was a great, gaping hole in my world when my
mentor died. It was all very sudden—she was diagnosed
and died all within the space of two months, and there
wasn't much time for any of us who loved her to adjust
to the idea of a world in which she just wasn't there
any longer. And then it came to me over the next
several weeks and months that she really is here, in a
way. I started doing a certain kind of investigative
writing after she died that was different from anything
I'd ever done before, but was very much along the lines
of what she herself found interesting. I would catch
myself asking the kinds of tricky, disarming questions
she delighted in asking during her interviews, questions
that elicited just the sort of information people are
usually so careful about not divulging.

There have been times when I've finished writing
a sentence and I'll recognize it as just the sort of
sentence she'd write—there's usually a telltale word or
turn of phrase she tended to use. There's also an irony
and an intelligence that I can't credit as being my own.
I don't want to say that I'm "channeling" her, or
anything silly like that; but I do sometimes feel that I'm
writing with her mind. It's a great feeling every time it

happens, just as, once in a while, I sometimes dream about her, and I always wake up feeling so pleased.

There was a certain doggedness about her that I so much admired, and in some ways I feel that I've been able to appropriate some of that discipline and determination and also a certain pleasure she took in small things. I don't know whether she really intended to bequeath any or all of this to me—it's her gift to all the younger writers who knew her, I guess. But whatever her intentions were, it's been a tremendous legacy.

Holding Ourselves to Higher Standards

Our mentors' belief in us is very much a sort of inspiration, in both the literal and figurative meanings of the word. Because our mentor expects great things of us, we are driven to achieve more than we would have without her belief in our potential. In a variation on CPR or "the kiss of life," our mentor also inspires us by filling us with her breath. She "exhales," as Tyler said at the end of chapter 6. She fills us with her words, as Marcella noted of her mentor. Like the older women of the tribe among our hunter-gatherer ancestors, our mentors sustain us and our hopes with the excess food and wisdom they've garnered. We are filled and fueled by this borrowed power. The only payback that's expected is our mentor's satisfaction at seeing us thrive.

Kirin talked about her mentor's generosity toward her, and how it's changed her outlook:

Sondra brought me with her in her rise up the corporate ladder—me and a couple of other people she knew she could count on. There was, sure, maybe a bit of empire building going on. But that didn't make it any less remarkable, the ascent upward. It doesn't make me any less grateful. I'm actually, right now, just at the level where she was when she first took an interest in my career. There's no way I could have risen so quickly without making a lateral move first to another company. It just doesn't work that way in business.

Because this has all happened in such a relatively short period of time, I've had to constantly be on my toes. I didn't want her to ever have to feel defensive about me, or to have to justify my promotions in any way apart from the quality of my work. It's made me subject all my major decisions at work to the most rigorous questioning—to try to see everything through her eyes as well as through my own.

Stephanie explained the way in which she's also internalized her mentor's point of view:

I did a student film, like everyone else at UCLA—the usual solipsistic, angst-ridden sort of thing. And later, when I was in my Ph.D. program, before I dropped out, I learned to see films in the bizarre way in which film scholars see them. But I didn't learn to see through the camera's eye until I started working with Dana.

She taught me how to tell a story through images; how every story, even a commercial, has to have a beginning, a middle, and an end. And I swear I think about this every time I look through the viewfinder. It can be just a nanosecond of association—but there's a sense in which her eyes are inside my head, and I see the shot as I know Dana would see it. This doesn't mean that I necessarily follow her vision rather than my own. I mean, I never do, not at this point. But I carry her around inside me like an extra pair of eyes.

Cathy spoke of a similar magic merge that took place between her and her mentor:

Sam's been retired for six years now, and there's a funny sense in which I feel like I've sort of stepped into her shoes. I find myself encouraging some of the new hires and younger secretaries in just the same way she encouraged me. This isn't the easiest thing in the world to admit, but there's a way in which she sort of passed on that whole Royal Family thing to me. I'm still me, and everything's more or less the same when I go back to Boston once a year to see my family—except now I have a lot of cash in my wallet and I'm wearing expensive, handmade Italian shoes. My mom swears every year that I'm getting taller. I just have to laugh then, because Sam was always telling me to stand up straight—and I guess I really do now, even though she's not around to remind me.

The presence of a mentor's voice inside us can sometimes make us wonder if we're coming up short in her eyes. There seems to be a split that takes place between the real mentor and the version of her we internalize. Hope noted how important it is to have frequent reality checks, if your mentor is around, to make sure that you're not imagining criticisms where none exist:

> *Because I chose to retire early and wasn't out there tilting at windmills anymore, I had assumed that she disapproved of the path I had taken. And I realized after a conversation with her that this was pure projection. It was obvious from the warmth in her voice; I felt certain that we were old friends again, and that felt so wonderful because we always had such a close, caring feeling about each other. I had felt quite hurt because I had imagined that she really wasn't living up to this great model of accepting other people's decision making, which I had always attributed to her. But she still does.*
>
> *It's so true in all human relationships. We build up pictures in our minds of what the other person is thinking, and we forget to check in to see if our picture has any match in reality. Often it doesn't. I never worked so hard in my life academically as I did when I was getting my Master's. But it was in some ways like I was someone who was starving to death, and then someone gave me an absolutely marvelous meal. That's how I think of those years when I studied with her.*

Caryn talked about similar feelings of self-doubt she's projected onto others:

> *I've experienced that with the mentors I've had, the fear that they were judging me, or the certainty that they were judging me, and that I would come up deficient. It's worse than imagining a parent's criticism, in a way, because your parent will always love you, and a mentor*

just doesn't come with that kind of unconditional warranty. But I also think that those kinds of fears have had more to do with my own issues than anything else. I think there's sometimes this tendency to feel convinced that your mentor thinks about you just as much as you think about yourself—and, of course, that's just not true.

Violetta discovered that it can sometimes be easier to accept any disappointment we may feel about our mentors than about ourselves:

I can think of one incident in particular where I felt that I'd disappointed her. It was an academic situation in which I felt that what I'd produced hadn't measured up to her opinion of me. I'd experienced feeling a sense of disappointment in her occasionally. But this was different, and it was even more painful in some ways.

Carol stressed her belief in the importance of not putting our mentors on too high a pedestal:

It may have something to do with the nature of my work as a psychologist, but I'm very wary about that sort of thing. In the relationship that I still have with my mentor, there's a certain honesty, and we both know that we have to work at the relationship.

    You can't completely insulate yourself from this kind of hurt; and there will, of course, be times when you don't connect with each other as well as you normally do, or you miscommunicate. But I think what's part and parcel with having a mentor is that the relationship goes beyond the surface of things, and you see that person—and hopefully yourself—blemishes and all. If you put someone on a pedestal, you're blinded, in that you only see their strengths. But like every other meaningful relationship, this type of relationship also has to have an honesty to it, and to be able to support a sense of vulnerability on the part of both of the people involved.

A mentor may pass on a general sense of high standards. Paula explained:

Pamela was in my life for a relatively short period of time, during a year and a half when I'd gotten completely fed up with things in this country and was living in the British Isles. I can't even point to one particular thing she taught me. In many ways, as a woman, as an artist, I think she felt a little trapped by her life, even though it was what would have been called a very good life by anyone's standards. She lived in a large and beautiful house in the English countryside. She had a whole flock of children, some of them grown and all of them fairly happy. Her husband was not only prominent in the government then, and hobnobbed with the Prime Minister, but he also clearly adored his wife and family.

She did a lot not only for her children, but also for the community. She had this huge organic garden that she let anyone work in, and of course she let them share in the harvest. She was always promoting animal rights and vegetarianism, and she even objected to the cultivation of cut flowers, as it used resources that could have been used to grow food.

I learned a ton of things about community and service and family by just living there during the weeks when I stayed at her house. And now, decades later, I hear her voice at the oddest times—when I'm making vinaigrette dressing, for one. She always called it "sour sauce." And when, once in a while, I bake bread, it always reminds me of the smell of her house and the way she was with her younger children.

We stayed in touch for a while; the last time I wrote to her was when her husband passed away. She never wrote back, and I don't even know if she's still alive. I wish I could tell her what it meant to me then, and how she's stayed with me after all these years—kind of a pocket mother, a psychic security blanket I can take out now and then. There aren't a lot of parallels between her life and mine. But knowing the way she was makes me want to be as good as I can be at what I do.

Part of Your Life for as Long as You Live

When you've made your decisions at the crossroads and you're on your chosen path, your mentor's role may evolve to that of extended family member or close family friend. You still care about each other. You're still grateful for all she's done. But you're not in the same place you were when you were so much in need of her help. Your relationship may become more reciprocal at this point; or she may continue to hover in the background of your life as an on-call advisor and cheering squad.

Most often, among the women I interviewed, mentors and their protégées seem to enjoy a till-death-do-us-part relationship, even though the nature of the relationship almost always evolves. Except in the case of poisonous mentorships—which we'll look at in chapter 9—there are no divorces, per se. Geography can keep our contacts few and far between. But, like old friends, we seem pretty much able to pick up the conversational thread where we left it the last time.

Charlotte spoke about her ongoing relationship with her mentor:

> *We still keep in touch. She'll write me notes. She's very good about keeping in touch with me on my birthday and that kind of thing. She's very conscientious in terms of just maintaining contact, so I always feel that sense that I can just pick up where we left off, which, I think, is kind of hard to maintain when you're long distance, you know? She's good at that. She keeps that level of support open to me all the time. And so it is kind of like family. I mean it's like she's just gonna be there, which I think is also rare with people in general, feeling like they're part of your life.*
>
> *Her value system was also part of her lasting influence on me, and it was really helpful. She decided that she had given enough of her time and energy to activism. She decided she'd done enough good for the world, and she wanted to do her art. It made me realize that activist work can be very draining, and that you really need to create a balance in your life. And she was doing that. She was balancing her creative side with*

her politics and her art. It always helps me in finding
that balance for myself to think of her.

Alejandra spoke about the ways in which her grandmother's influence in her teenage years continues to hearten
her:

I'm thirty-five now, and I think it's because of her that
I don't so much mind the idea of getting older. You
know, when I turned thirty, I felt a little bit panicked.
I found myself at the cosmetics counter at Macy's, trying
out a lot of different creams for my skin. But when
I think about my grandmother, it makes me feel okay
about getting older, because she is a person who has
kept growing, you know? And getting wiser and even
more beautiful, in a way. Even as an old person, she
has a very open mind.

Rita said that she often hears her aunt's voice, "with
her strong Welsh accent, of course!" A mentor's influence,
even that of one long gone, can be something we carry
around us like an aura.

Dorothy feels that everything she is today, and all the
happiness she finds in her marriage, her two children, her
friendships, and, most recently, her writing, are a sort of
blessing conferred on her half a century ago by her grandmother's determination and love:

My primary mentor is, or was, my grandmother.
I think through my entire life, though, I've had a lot
of mentors—angels that stepped into my life at the very
time I needed them. Whomever I needed, or whatever
I needed, it seemed it was provided for me right at the

*time that it was important for that person to appear.
But my grandmother is the one who came first and did
the most for me. She stepped in and really saved my life
when I was three years old and in danger of becoming a
lost child, because my own parents were simply unable to
care for me.*

There are some people who believe that we meet pre-
cisely the right people in life who can teach us the lessons
we need to learn. Paula said:

*I think it's this way with the relationships we have,
even if they're in the end very negative relationships that
we have to end. We're confronted with all the issues we
most need to work through. It's the same with the
children who are born to us or whom we find to
adopt—we have something special and particular that
they need, and they are just the right children to teach
us what we most need to learn, even if that learning
process is very, very painful sometimes. And this is also
true, I think, for the mentors that life delivers to us,
and that's why, for the important ones, their influence
stays with us throughout our lives.*

In her essay "Anna O./Bertha Pappenheim and Me,"
filmmaker Ann H. Jackowitz writes of a completely acci-
dental meeting that changed the course of her career:
"After class, over coffee with a group of people, I met a
woman who was working on a film project.... Her background was neither film nor history nor psychology, but
she was determined, and I admired that. This chance
encounter with a total stranger changed my life" (254).

Marcella has much the same feeling about her relationship with her mentor, which sprang from an informal encounter:

> *There's no doubt in my mind that my life was profoundly changed by meeting her, having her take such a shine to my work, and having the privilege of spending time with her over the remaining four years of her life.*
>
> *Maybe I would have carved out this career for myself anyway. But maybe without the validation and encouragement she gave me, I would have just given up and gone back to editing and corporate writing and looking at fiction and nonfiction as something I would always have to do on the side. I still draw on her strength and her wit and the tremendous sense in which she was always ready to stand up for something or someone she believed in.*

Old Mentors Never Die (They Live Forever Inside Us)

Our mentors are most often older than we are. If the relationship lasts sufficiently long, or if it begins near the end of her life, we will very likely be faced someday with our mentor's death.

Much has been written elsewhere on the pain of losing one's own mother. When your mentor is your mother, you are faced with a double loss—you lose both your progenitor and your guide. But there is a very real sense in which your mother lives on in you. You are the fulfillment of her greatest biological urge: through you, her genetic blueprint lives on after her death. If she has taught and nurtured you well, she will also live on in what you give forth to the world of her kindness and wisdom.

Our mentors who are not blood relatives achieve a psychic immortality in everything we accomplish and in every bit of encouragement, validation, and hope we are able to pass on, in our turn, to the next generation. What our mentors do for us is not easily forgotten.

Leah, who is in her seventies now, spoke with emotion about the modest Englishwoman who saved her from the Nazis when she was fourteen:

> *I owe my life to Mabel. I always say that my middle name is grateful. I owe every breath I take to her. I have some regrets that I never fully told her this. A lot of the feelings between us went unspoken; and after I moved away to the States, and married and had children, I was too distracted. We saw each other a few times. She visited me and also a sister she had here, and she was so delighted with my children. But I very much wish I had thought or taken the time to tell her, to say, "Thank you, Mabel."*

There seems to be a sense in which a mentor takes up permanent residence inside us, whether or not she's still alive. Marcella told me that she keeps a scrap of cloth from a shawl she made for her mentor, and touches it when she wants to connect with her again.

Jordan feels that she's still able to communicate with her mother:

> *I write letters to her in a journal every day. I'm so grateful for the mom I had and for all her wisdom. It*

seems like I've started doing things with my kids that I remember her doing with us. Sometimes I just see myself as her. When those words come out of your mouth that she said to you, and then you hear yourself saying those same words to your kids, you think, "Oh my God, I sound like my mom." But I think it's great that I do. There's so much of who I am that I got from her.

She's buried in the cemetery, and I go up there all the time. Any time some of my sisters do something they're not supposed to, I go tell on them—"Mom, they're acting up. They ain't acting right." The one thing I know is that I always feel I can still talk to her, and I know she listens to me. She's the foundation of my foundation.

9

*When the
Mentor-Protégée
Relationship Goes Awry*

It's maybe what you could call narcissistic mentoring. As long as you're admiring her, and agreeing with everything she says, you know, everything's good. But when you start to step back and she starts to bite into you, she can be very mean.

—Charlotte

You still have to keep your own mind in a relationship with a mentor. No matter how much you look up to her or trust her, you can't give your power over to this person, because she may make a bad decision for you at some point.

—Paula

I was a fly caught in a web, and the spider was my mentor.

—Deirdre

Because the connection between a mentor and her protégée is so profound, the stakes are high. Any relationship that partakes so freely of the emotional complexity of the mother-daughter bond is bound to be tricky for both people involved. We're vulnerable to our mentors, just as we're vulnerable to our mothers. Both can buoy us with their approval or devastate us with an expression of disappointment in us.

Paula talked about the complexity of these relationships:

> *I've noticed that most of my female clients, no matter how old they are or what they do in life, have an intense and abiding desire to have their mother's approval—even if they don't like their mother! On some level, it's very difficult for any woman or girl to feel good about herself without the belief that she's worthy in her mother's eyes, no matter what she's accomplished. If Mom is absent or ungiving, we look to other people for the unconditional love that a mother is supposed to give us. The trouble is that, outside the mother- child bond, love is almost always conditional.*

It would be irresponsible not to examine the negative as well as the positive aspects of the mentor-protégée bond. Just as you can get your heart broken when you fall in love, there is the possibility of getting burned when you look to a mentor for guidance and validation.

The happy stories by far outnumber the unhappy ones: most of the women I interviewed had only good things to say about the relationship and what it has meant to their lives. Betsy said:

> *I can't really say that I've had a lot of fear of disapproval, maybe because I never had any kind of mentorship for a very long time. My experience has been that, once I found a mentor in any given person, I was so glad to have a relationship where I was learning and blossoming and so on. But I always just assumed it would go well and continue to be positive. I never had much experience to the contrary.*

Many women, like Betsy, have an unclouded experience with their mentor. But what happens when the mentor-protégée relationship goes awry?

A Basketful of Apples

In "Snow White," the wicked queen disguises herself as an old peddler to gain entrance to the seven dwarves' cottage and be in a position to put an end to her young rival's reign as fairest in the land. In one such foray, she tempts Snow White with a basketful of apples. Only one half of one of these ripe fragrant apples is poisoned.

Life offers us a basketful of mentors to choose from. Odds are, we'll probably be lucky in our choices. But there is a slight possibility that, like Snow White, we'll be most drawn to the single apple in the basket that's been laced with poison.

Reading the fairy tale, girls may feel frustrated at Snow White's naivete. How could she fall for that stupid disguise? Why can't she follow the simple instruction the dwarves left her with: *Don't open the door!* Again and again, Snow White gives in to the temptations the wicked queen offers her.

It's Snow White's particular need for a mother's loving attention that makes her so vulnerable. The wicked queen offers nurture in the form of the apples. She offers Snow White help in making the transition from girl to woman by enticing her with pretty combs for her hair and laces that will accentuate her womanly curves. Because Snow White has never gotten this type of help—her mother died when she was born—she is hungry for the emotional food the queen, in the guise of the peddler, dangles before her. Her need clouds her judgment, so that she doesn't consider whether there might be poison in the apples or the combs. It never occurs to her that her rival might try to strangle her with the pretty laces. Snow White's vulnerability makes her ignore the good advice her friends give her. She fails to see her own vulnerability and its effects on her judgment. And she also fails to question what merely seem to be gestures of kindness from a benign older woman.

The neediness we feel when we first meet our mentor can dictate how far we have to fall if things go sour. Some women just seem to be more naturally cautious than others, always keeping the inner core of who they are safe from violation. Betsy tends toward the cautious side:

> *I can't say that I had great fears in that area, although I'd heard my mentor be harsh about other people. I was certainly aware that she was capable of being harsh. I was delighted whenever I had her approval, and wanted it and so on, but I can't say that I feared anything in particular. I think I just operated carefully to try to make sure nothing would go wrong. That's just part of who I am, and I think it*

*might have made me keep just a little bit of distance,
in some ways.*

Mentors with Agendas, Chips on Their Shoulder, or Axes to Grind

Bad mentor experiences can run the range from mildly unpleasant to truly awful memories that leave life-long scars. Charlotte found that she ran into trouble when she overidealized one of her professors in graduate school. The relationship was satisfying until Charlotte started questioning her mentor's judgment and motivations:

*I had a bad mentor experience with a professor when
I was getting my Master's in Social Work. She was an
activist, and she inspired pretty strong emotions in people:
they either really loved her or really hated her. She had
a very strong personality, and she was very harsh. At
that time, I was in a phase of my life where I felt ready
to put myself to the test. I'd heard so much about her.
People had really idealized her, and I was sucked in
from the beginning to idealize her, too. She's also a
person of color, and I'm white, so there was a certain
amount of idealizing, on my part, about the wisdom
possessed by people of color—that kind of thing. I mean
there's all sorts of weird stuff that I think, later on,
came out for me.*

*She was an incredibly brilliant teacher. Our
relationship soon got beyond that teacher-student mode.
She selected out a few kids—students, I should say—
who would come to her house for special occasions. After*

I finished my program, I developed more of a long-term relationship with her and her partner. But after a while she kind of unleashed this little critical thing on me. It was like I wasn't activist enough. I wasn't this enough, my job wasn't cool enough or it was too mainstream. I wasn't breaking down the social barriers or really taking down the system. And, of course, I was so ready to eat that up, because I was feeling so guilty that I had grown up privileged and white in a well-off family. It was that sort of dynamic where I was ready to just accept whatever she had to say to me. I also tend to be kind of self-critical, so it was this very strong thing, between her criticisms of me and my criticisms of myself.

I finally had to just push back from her, because I realized, this isn't about me. You know, this is really about her being somewhat of a bully and a perfectionist, and I've seen her do it to other people, too, where she can be kind of manipulative of people's egos. She can be judgmental and not very supportive. She has these very high expectations that are not connected to the reality of what people have to face when they go into the work world. You have to survive and make a living, and you may end up having to compromise your values at times. You may have to work for institutions that you don't totally agree with if you're going to do other things to make a living; and she wouldn't accept that. That was not acceptable to her, and it was as if it was our fault. As she saw it, we hadn't tried hard enough. We hadn't created the job that was really consistent with our values.

I think she took her politics one step too far away from the heart. It's maybe what you could call

> *narcissistic mentoring. As long as you're admiring her,*
> *and agreeing with everything she says, you know,*
> *everything's good. But when you start to step back and*
> *she starts to bite into you, she can be very mean.*

Joyce had an experience that was similar to Charlotte's, although it happened outside the academic world:

> *We had what seemed like a perfectly beautiful*
> *relationship—it was a real love fest every time we saw*
> *each other. Here she was this highly regarded person in*
> *her late seventies, almost worshipped, really, among a*
> *certain contingent of people in her field. And then it*
> *just suddenly shifted, and she became an enemy and*
> *a torturer. It was pretty horrendous, and it made me*
> *very cautious about entering into that kind of*
> *relationship again, because I felt so hurt.*

While we appreciate the ways in which our mentors
push us to do our best, we also look to them to nurture and
protect us. It can be a terrible shock to find that a mentor's
advice is actually harming us. Terry talked about an experience with her gymnastics coach, who had become her role
model and mentor:

> *Going into the twelfth grade, I injured my back in a*
> *very serious way during a practice. I still have medical*
> *repercussions from that injury, nearly twenty-five years*
> *later. But I think my coach never really believed that*
> *my back was injured. So that's where it kind of sours,*
> *because I was still competing and pushing myself, but*
> *I was really in a lot of pain. Subsequently, I realized*
> *I should have just stopped. She completely failed to*

support me at all in this. When I would try to talk with her about the injury, she just didn't want to hear about it.

I don't know what would make her think that I would make something like that up or somehow fake an injury. It's not like I had a track record of blowing things out of proportion. It was a really serious injury, but for a year I kept competing. Every day, I did gymnastics, to the point where it was so painful. And in the end I couldn't take the scholarship I was offered.

Then the addendum was that I have this sister who is two years younger than I am but three years younger in school. She came up behind me in gymnastics, and she was even more of a star than I was, and so she was even bigger on Mrs. Watkins' radar screen than I had been. So there I was at a college I didn't even really want to go to, because I couldn't take the scholarship I was offered; and there was my sister having this even better life with Mrs. Watkins, who I had idealized and admired so much. It really felt like a betrayal.

Maybe she'd just gone into denial about my injury because she didn't want to face it. But then for her to turn her back on me, really, and turn her attention to my sister! That really hurt. My sister is a super athlete. She went on to teach and coach gymnastics, and she and Mrs. Watkins were even professional colleagues at one point.

Thinking about it now, it doesn't have the same impact for me. But for a number of years, it was a really painful thing to hear all these stories my sister would tell—ugh! Every time I'd hear stories about

> *Mrs. Watkins, I don't know, it just hurt. I don't blame my sister. But, you know, I don't like Mrs. Watkins anymore.*

Paula talked about how she thinks we can protect ourselves from being devastated by a failed mentor-protégée relationship:

> *You still have to keep your own mind in a relationship with a mentor. No matter how much you look up to her or trust her, you can't give your power over to this person, because she may make a bad decision for you at some point. It's a real pitfall in this type of relationship, because the power is unevenly shared between the two people involved.*
>
> *You don't want to put your emotional well-being into anyone else's hands, whether we're talking about a mentor or a lover or a husband or even a beloved child. To be emotionally healthy, each of us has to carry that sense of well-being inside us. The moment you give it away to someone else, the way things turn out is completely out of your control—and it may take you a while to get back to the place where you were before entering into this relationship. In extreme cases, you may never get back there again, because the damage is simply too great, and you'll have a lot of trouble trusting other people or making yourself vulnerable again by loving someone.*

Although Ursula found a powerful role model and mentor in her mother, the effects of this relationship on each of them weren't always positive:

There's always a double edge to these things. One of the double edges to this relationship with my mom is that in following her around, and trying to be like her in many ways, I think she felt very crowded. Because she was quite a young mother, she hadn't had time to explore or ever really be on her own. And as I grew up, I think she envied the options that were open to me. As I became more adventurous and there were more and more things I was doing, I think she felt a little jealous.

I became an adolescent in the sixties—and my sisters did, too—at the time when the Pill had just been popularized. We all got on it, and we all had sexual experiences. And my mother suddenly shortened her skirts. She was forty, she was happily married, and she flirted shamelessly with my boyfriends and with my sisters' boyfriends, and my father acted as if that was fine. He liked my mother's sort of crudity. I mean, my mother wasn't acting on it. She was just in some unconscious ways very seductive, but I think that there was a big, unacknowledged envy that we had the opportunity to experiment and to be with others that she hadn't. And so one of the symptoms of this was that she was always trying to outshine me.

Where we had difficulty again was when I started to go in some different directions artistically. When I started to get into some shows and take off in my own direction, she didn't like that. And she didn't want me to see her failures. So all of that was happening in addition to the usual Oedipal things going on there, where I'm feeling a little guilty toward my mother because I'm really close to my dad. I want to be like

> *my mother, I don't want to hurt her, but I probably do*
> *unconsciously want to remove her so that I can have my*
> *father for myself. And my mother's slightly aware of*
> *this. She's also aware as she's aging and in her forties*
> *that my sexual future is before me. I have choices she*
> *didn't have. And she's feeling pushed out of the way*
> *a little.*
>
> *The negative aspects of this creep up in strange*
> *ways. We once did a piece together that was in an*
> *important gallery show, and she just sort of "forgot" to*
> *have the gallery owner include my name in the catalogue.*

It's difficult to be objective when we first fall into a relationship with a mentor. It's generally the furthest thing from our mind to wonder just why this marvelous person has taken such a shine to us. And there may be no reason other than her very healthy interest in furthering our growth or our career. She may very well simply like us. But sometimes there are other factors involved, factors that most often have little or nothing to do with us.

Some of these factors can be present without doing the relationship any harm. Simone, for instance, is aware that her first mentor had a frustrating relationship with her own daughter, who was a little bit older than Simone:

> *I think I was kind of what her daughter should have*
> *been, because I was listening to her, because I was doing*
> *all the right things that a daughter sometimes cannot do.*
> *I could never have that kind of relationship with my*
> *mother. I couldn't listen to her, because I thought that*
> *everything she was doing was wrong. So in this way my*
> *mentor and I were able to provide something for each*

> *other that sprang out of a lack or a need that each of us had.*

Most often, a mentor's lack or need, such as the one described by Simone, will not interfere with the positive exchange in a mentor-protégée relationship. But when such a need is the fuel for the relationship as well as the reason why it started, there is the potential for things to go wrong.

Joyce talked about how her relationship with her mentor went awry because of a factor she failed to see at its outset:

> *I was vain or needy enough to allow myself to believe that this famous and fascinating person was giving me entrée to her life because she found me utterly captivating. I found out, years later, after I'd undertaken to become her official biographer and was in a very entrenched relationship with her, that I'm a dead-ringer for her eldest daughter, who is manic depressive, and with whom she had a very troubled relationship. She actually raised this girl telling her all along that she was adopted, when, really, she was her biological child. It was very complicated, and very sad for both the mother and the daughter. So here I waltzed into her life looking like a healthier, perhaps a more successful version of this daughter she loved very much but also felt very guilty toward. As far as I understand it, theirs was very much an on-again, off-again, love-hate relationship.*
>
> *I don't even know if she consciously made this connection between me and her daughter, although her sister—who is someone I tremendously admire—said she must have. She says the resemblance is just astonishing.*

So I occupied the position of privileged friend for a couple of pretty blissful years. She was getting on in years, and she was in poor health and taking a lot of medications; and she was drinking, too. I went off to Europe for half a year, actually with the express purpose of visiting the various places where she'd lived there; but perhaps she felt that I shouldn't have gone away for such a long time, because she was in quite poor health then.

When I returned, I was exposed to the hate part of the relationship. She actually became emotionally abusive with me, doing her best to humiliate me in front of other people—and she did this quite effectively. I had just gotten out of an abusive marriage. And so here was this person I cared for so much and whom I admired so much suddenly abusing me. It was really dreadful.

The experience made me a little fearful in the next mentor-protégée relationship I got into. And that turned out, thank God, where we were still friends when she died. It was a very wonderful relationship. But at every turn I was afraid of it turning poisonous or having her reveal that she thought nothing of me, or that I would suddenly do something to turn her against me. I was very gun-shy about that up until the end.

Tyler, who says that she has all her illusions intact vis-à-vis her mentor, can nonetheless understand how a mentor-protégée relationship can unravel if it's based on fantasy or projection:

When the romantic bubble bursts and you see that they're alcoholics or they have this terrible relationship with their past or whatever it is, and they're totally in denial about it. . . . It's like falling in love with someone and at first, he's the most fabulous person on earth. But then you live together for a while, or there's some kind of new stress or change in your life, and you say, "Oh, my God, I didn't see this before." And you start to see their difficulties and their faults and when they're not going to come through for you, and it's very painful, because there's so much invested.

And the choice at that point is, do I stay in this faulty, fault-ridden relationship, or do I get out? And, do the rewards outweigh the painful things about it? Or do you accept the flaws and take what you can get from it, in spite of them?

When the Magic Mirror Is Cracked

The overwhelming number of mentor-protégée relationships are life-enhancing in every way. But occasionally one hears of a mentor who follows in the footsteps of the evil stepmothers and wicked witches of fairy tales.

At the age of twenty, Deirdre, who is now a professional singer, was taken under the wing of Solange, an older European musician. Solange gave her music lessons and introduced Deirdre to her circle of friends. Deirdre, who had never had a boyfriend and felt alienated from her parents, soon became entangled in a ménage à trois with Solange and her husband. The two nurtured Deirdre and launched her on her professional career while exploiting her for their own pleasure.

Deirdre recognizes both the good and the bad that Solange gave her over the three and a half years of their relationship:

My life was on a road that dramatically changed direction when Solange came into my life. I went from naive to sophisticated, from provincial to worldly, from small-time to big-time.

Solange and I stayed fairly close until she died, about ten years ago. But it is only since then that I have really come into my own. I raised my child, got an advanced degree, got a great job, and continue to practice my art. Did that episode hurt me? I don't know. I still find it hard to trust completely. I was a fly caught in a web, and the spider was my mentor. I loved her, and she gave me a life I never would've had. She gave love and withdrew it again, keeping me off-balance, eager to please, angry, and confused. I still have a certain fear of being vulnerable. I have never married. I am, however, very much at peace with myself.

I feel like I learned some invaluable lessons about how I want my life to be from my relationship with her. Solange had a terrible fear of aging. I don't have that. I'm enjoying getting older, because I feel myself getting wiser.

10

Completing the Circle

When I thanked her, she said, "A lot of people have opened doors for me over the years. If I can open a door for you, it'll just be a way of completing the circle."

—*Stephanie*

Women especially, I think, are recognizing the virtues of cooperation and information sharing, because we're starting to get an inkling of the positive changes we can make in the world.

—*Marcella*

Now I'm in a position where people are looking to me to be mentored, because I'm the teacher and they're the student. There's a tremendous responsibility that goes along with being a mentor. I remember how much influence my mentors had over me.

—*Lori*

One of the rewards of graduating from the school of hard knocks is a fund of knowledge that's yours to save or spend, depending on your outlook on life. Some people hold the attitude that everyone needs to learn life's lessons the hard way. Others delight in easing the passage of those who come after them.

Stephanie spoke of the generosity of one of her mentors toward her:

> *I called up a professor of mine years after I'd graduated from film school, because I'd seen her byline on a film review in the newspaper, and I was just at that time thinking that I'd like to start reviewing films myself. She told me everything she could think of that might get the editor to take me seriously, and she said I could use her name if I thought that would help. When I thanked her, she said, "A lot of people have opened doors for me over the years. If I can open a door for you, it'll just be a way of completing the circle."*

There are plenty of people who don't want to open the doors of opportunity too wide, for fear of the competition that might crowd them. Others, like Stephanie's professor, feel safe enough in their abilities to know that there is ample room in every field for as many high-quality people who want to enter. Instead of feeling threatened by a younger or newer person's excellence, they feel glad that the general standards around them will be raised. Like the queen in our revisionist version of "Snow White," they will exult in the success of the younger people they've been able to nurture and nudge into full bloom.

A Giant Web of Support

One of the pleasures of getting older is the chance to help and encourage younger people (as we continue to give pep talks to ourselves and our contemporaries). Among the many lessons our mentors teach us by example is how to be a mentor. There are books and articles on how to be a mentor, but perhaps the best way to learn this wonderful, life-giving skill is to be the recipient of it at one time or another. It's never too late to find a mentor; and it's never too late to become one.

Susan Caminiti writes in *Working Woman*, "The simple act of teaching, by sharing stories and experiences, has been going on since men in loincloths swapped hunting tales. What's different is how women are redefining its role in the workplace to fulfill their particular needs" (62).

In the same article, Caminiti quotes Gail Graham, a thirty-nine-year-old bank executive, who says that because of her mentor and the women she met through her, she feels like she has "a giant web of support." Graham continued: "So often you think you're the only one going through something, but now I feel like I can fall and land in the web and things will be okay" (63).

Paula expanded on this idea:

> *I think of the link between a mentor and her protégée as the smallest unit in a larger web of supportiveness, empathy, and nurturing that may eventually show itself to be the world's safety net. If what you've learned in your life can help another person learn more quickly, then the learning curve of the world's emotional intelligence will begin to slant upwards. If you can use*

*any of the keys on your key ring to open doors that will
allow other people to speed themselves on in their personal
evolution, then the world's locked doors of potential will
begin flying open. If we each share what we know, the
earth will grow wiser much faster than if everyone has to
keep learning everything all over again on his or her
own.*

Fairy Godmother as Career Path

Is it possible to even conceive of a society in which wisdom
is esteemed just as highly as youth and beauty? When our
time to play Cinderella passes, can we joyfully step into the
sparkling shoes of the fairy godmother?

Lori, as a teacher, is beginning to understand the
power that comes with wearing those shoes: "Now I'm in a
position where people are looking to me to be mentored,
because I'm the teacher and they're the student. There's a
tremendous responsibility that goes along with being a
mentor. I remember how much influence my mentors had
over me."

Fairy godmothers have, by definition, arrived at their
career goal: they are fully empowered to work their magic
to help others. Their job description reads, "Live in the
world as a beneficent presence that will help others actual-
ize their dreams. Wake the Sleeping Beauties of the world,
replace Cinderella's rags with fine clothes and send her to
life's ball, remove the piece of poisoned apple from Snow
White's throat so that she can wake to her own happiness."

Cathy spoke about the ways in which she now feels
able to expand the legacy of her mentor:

Sam helped me so much, and now I'm in a position to help other, younger women coming into the firm. And it's not just at work that I can pass on what Sam gave to me. There must be half a dozen opportunities every day wherever I interact with other people—on the subway, at restaurants, at the grocery store, or just walking down the street—when I can slip in an encouraging smile or a compliment and change someone's day. Believe me, I know what a difference that stuff can make. We think of it as throwaway stuff, but it's gold and jewels that we scatter to the world. I'm only in a position to share it with others because of the great gift of abundance that Sam gave to me. I can afford to give it away, because that well is never going to run dry again.

How To Live Forever

Changing lives in a positive way, or making the world a better place to live in, is an even more certain path to immortality than giving birth to a child. As women, we're uniquely equipped to do both.

For centuries, most women have not had the time, opportunities, or resources to focus their energies on world improvement. In the twentieth century, we had more leisure time, at least in the western industrialized world, to think about more than survival—and many of us set about a course of improving the quality of our own individual lives.

Marcella spoke with passion about the collective consciousness communicated to her by her mentor:

*One of the things she taught me in the way she lived
her own life was to try to see the larger picture—to get
beyond the whole idea of our own little family to the
family of humankind. I think a lot of people now,
myself included, are hungry for some meaning beyond
getting ahead in our work or just being a success or
making money. We're finding more room in our embrace
beyond the room we've always made there for our own
children or members of our immediate family. Women
especially, I think, are recognizing the virtues of
cooperation and information sharing, because we're
starting to get an inkling of the positive changes we can
make in the world.*

As women grow used to their wings, testing their
strength and power, they are also discovering the warmth
and space those wings allow to nurture and embolden
whatever fledglings venture underneath them.

References

Adams-Ender, Clara L. 1991. "Mentoring: Nurses Helping Nurses." *RN,* April, 54:4.

Angier, Natalie. 1999. *Woman: An Intimate Geography.* Boston and New York: Houghton Mifflin Company.

Bergen, D.J., and J.E. Williams. 1991. "Sex Stereotypes in the United States Revisited: 1972–1991." *Sex Roles,* 24:413–23.

Bern, S.L. 1974. "The Measurement of Psychological Androgyny." *Journal of Consulting and Clinical Psychology* 42:155–62. In *Women and Work: A Reader,* edited by Paula J. Dubeck and Kathryn Borman. 1997. New Brunswick, N.J.: Rutgers University Press.

Bettelheim, Bruno. 1989. *The Uses of Enchantment: The Meaning and Importance of Fairy Tales.* New York: Vintage Books.

Caminiti, Susan. 1999. "Straight Talk." *Working Woman,* September, v24 n8:66–69.

Caplan, Paula J. 1989. *Don't Blame Mother: Mending the Mother-Daughter Relationship.* New York: Harper and Row.

Cavender, Cathy. 1990. "Networking News: The One-Minute Mentor." *Working Woman,* July, v15 n7:13.

Chevigny, Bell Gale. 1993. "Daughters Writing: Toward a Theory of Women's Biography." In *Between Women,* edited by Carol Ascher, Louise DeSalvo, and Sara Ruddick. New York and London: Routledge.

Chodorow, Nancy, and Susan Contratto. 1978. *The Reproduction of Mothering: Psychoanalysis and the Sociology of Gender.* Berkeley: University of California Press.

Cook, E.D. 1985. *Psychological Androgyny.* New York: Pergamon. Cited in *Women and Work: A Reader,* edited by Paula J. Dubeck and Kathryn Borman. 1997. New Brunswick, N.J.: Rutgers University Press.

Cox, Fran, and Louis Cox. 1990. *A Conscious Life: Cultivating the Seven Qualities of Authentic Adulthood.* Berkeley: Conari Press.

Diamond, Jared. 1996. "Why Women Change." *Discover,* July, vol.17, no.7, p.130.

Feuerwerker, Yi-Tsi Mei. 1993. "In Quest of Ding Ling (In Quest of Myself)." In *Between Women,* edited by Carol Ascher, Louise DeSalvo, and Sara Ruddick. New York and London: Routledge.

Fort, Deborah C., Stephanie J. Bird, and Catherine J. Didion, eds. 1993. *A Hand Up: Women Mentoring Women in Science.* Washington, D.C.: Association for Women in Science. Cited in *Women and Work: A Reader*, edited by Paula J. Dubeck and Kathryn Borman. 1997. New Brunswick, N.J.: Rutgers University Press.

Gibbons, Ann. 1993. "White Men Can Mentor: Help from the Majority." *Science*, November, v262 n5136:1130.

Goleman, Daniel. 1995. *Emotional Intelligence: Why It Can Matter More than IQ.* New York: Bantam Books.

Jackowitz, Ann H. 1993. "Anna O./Bertha Pappenheim and Me." In *Between Women,* edited by Carol Ascher, Louise DeSalvo, and Sara Ruddick. New York and London: Routledge.

Kingma, Daphne Rose. 1987. *Coming Apart: Why Relationships End and How to Live Through the Ending of Yours.* Berkeley: Conari Press.

Kohut, Hans. 1971. *The Analysis of the Self: A Systematic Approach to the Psychoanalytic Treatment of Narcissistic Personality Disorder.* New York: International Universities Press, Inc.

Lazarre, Jane. 1989. "'Charlotte's Web': Reading *Jane Eyre* Over Time." In *Between Women,* edited by Carol Ascher, Louise DeSalvo, and Sara Ruddick. New York and London: Routledge.

Leslie, Diane. 1999. *Fleur de Leigh's Life of Crime.* New York: Simon & Schuster.

Lueptow, Lloyd B. 1997. "Sex Stereotypes: An Underlying Dimension." In *Women and Work: A Reader,* edited by Paula J. Dubeck and Kathryn Borman. 1997. New Brunswick, N.J.: Rutgers University Press.

Lueptow, Lloyd B., and L. Garovich. 1992. "The Persistence of Sex Stereotypes amid the Reconstruction of Woman's Role." Paper presented at the annual meeting of the American Sociological Association, Pittsburgh, Pennsylvania, August 1992. Cited in *Women and Work: A Reader,* edited by Paula J. Dubeck and Kathryn Borman. 1997. New Brunswick, N.J.: Rutgers University Press.

Matclynski, T., and K. Comer 1991. "Mentoring Women and Minorities: An Anecdotal Record." Dayton, Ohio: University of Dayton, Department of Education. Cited in *Women and Work: A Reader,* edited by Paula J. Dubeck and Kathryn Borman. 1997. New Brunswick, N.J.: Rutgers University Press.

Menges, Robert, and William Exum. 1983. "Barriers to the Progress of Women and Minority Faculty." *Journal of Higher Education,* 33(2). Cited in *Women and Work: A Reader,* edited by Paula J. Dubeck and Kathryn Borman. 1997. New Brunswick, N.J.: Rutgers University Press.

Minnich, Elizabeth Kamarck. 1989. "Hannah Arendt: Thinking as We Are." In *Between Women,* edited by Carol Ascher, Louise DeSalvo, and Sara Ruddick. New York and London: Routledge.

National Mentoring Partnership web site. Available at www.mentoring.org; INTERNET.

Simon, R.J., and J.M. Landis. 1989. "Women's and Men's Attitudes about a Woman's Place and Role." *Public Opinion Quarterly,* 53:265–76. Cited in *Women and Work: A Reader,* edited by Paula J. Dubeck and Kathryn Borman. 1997. New Brunswick, N.J.: Rutgers University Press.

Soukhanov, Anne H. (exec. ed.) *American Heritage Dictionary of the English Language,* Third Edition. 1992. Boston: Houghton Mifflin Company.

Thorne, B., and M. Yalom (eds). 1982. "The Fantasy of the Perfect Mother" in *Rethinking the Family: Some Feminist Questions.* New York: Longman.

Williams, J.E., and D.L. Best. 1990. *Measuring Sex Stereotypes: A Multinational Study.* Revised ed. Newbury Park, Calif.: Sage. Cited in *Women and Work: A Reader,* edited by Paula J. Dubeck and Kathryn Borman. 1997. New Brunswick, N.J.: Rutgers University Press.

Photo by Donald E. McIlraith

Barbara Quick is a writer, poet, dancer, and the author of *Still Friends: Living Happily Ever After . . . Even if Your Marriage Falls Apart* and *Northern Edge: A Novel of Survival in Alaska's Arctic.* She writes frequently for the *New York Times Book Review* and has published essays and articles in *Newsweek, Ms.,* the *Los Angeles Times,* and *People Magazine.* She lives in the San Francisco Bay Area and is currently working on her second novel.

More New Harbinger Titles

GOODBYE GOOD GIRL

Good girls know all the rules that dictate what's becoming for a woman to be and do. The dozens of women whose stories are told in this book confirmed what authors Eileen Clegg and Susan Swartz learned from their own experience: it may be scary to challenge the rules, but the results can be astonishing, inspiring, and well worth the struggle.   *Item GGG $12.95*

CLAIMING YOUR CREATIVE SELF

Shares the inspiring stories of women who were able to keep in touch with their creative spirit and let it lead them to a place in their lives where something truly magical is taking place.   *Item CYCS $15.95*

WOMEN'S SEXUALITIES

A well-known sex educator and therapist uses stories and results derived from her breakthrough sexuality survey to show readers how to accept and enhance their sexuality.   *Item WOSE $15.95*

AFTER THE BREAKUP

A diverse sample of straight, lesbian, and bisexual women of all ages speak out about what really happens when couplehood ends and offer fresh perspectives on how to rebuild your identity and enjoy a life filled with new possibilities.   *Item ATB $13.95*

PERIMENOPAUSE

This self-care guide helps women cope with symptoms and assure health and vitality in the years ahead.   *Item PERI $16.95*

HIGH ON STRESS

Helps women rethink the role of stress in their lives, rework their physical and mental responses to it, and find ways to boost the potentially positive impact that stress can have on their well-being.   *Item HOS $13.95*

Call toll-free 1-800-748-6273 to order. Have your Visa or Mastercard number ready. Or send a check for the titles you want to New Harbinger Publications, 5674 Shattuck Avenue, Oakland, CA 94609. Include $3.80 for the first book and 75¢ for each additional book to cover shipping and handling. (California residents please include appropriate sales tax.) Allow four to six weeks for delivery.

Prices subject to change without notice.